YOU ARE

a spiritual being having a human experience.

YOU ARE NOT

your body, your business or your bank account.

YOU ARE

from the Unknown, of the Unseen, for the Unlimited.

from fear to faith:

10 Steps on the Spiritual Path of the Entrepreneur

marlo rencher

MendeMedia

Detroit

To my family –
past, present and future –
from the Mende to Mali.
Let the circle be unbroken.

Acknowledgements

This book was created for entrepreneurs, by an entrepreneur. It is a product of my passions – to invent a world connected with Spirit, to give people access to their "next level," and to embrace both fear and faith.

I accept full responsibility for the flaws in this text. Its virtues are the result of the support of too many people to name. I shall, however, make my best attempt.

Thank you…

To Lisa Nicole Hankerson for inspiring me to write this book by first writing her own – *The Key Party*. I also thank my friend, her husband Tony Hankerson, for lending a listening ear and occasionally a shoulder to cry on.

To Norma Jenkins and Robert Jenkins, Sr., for their steadfast parenting, unconditional love and abiding friendship. I love you both – and I really like you too :-)! Thank you for creating the structure for me to succeed!

To Robert Jenkins, Jr., for being the best brother, ever. You are my favorite person and the funniest man I know.

To my family, in Detroit, Chicago and all around the world. Shout outs to the Andrews, Bates, Bishops, Chatmans, Coles, Conrads, Ellises, Fambros, Hughes, Jenkins, Moores, Ruffs, Schlickers, Travises, Virgils, Wests, Williams and everyone else. Thank you for your prayers, support and encouragement.

To my mentor Jim Robinson for teaching me about entrepreneurship and faith.

To Vivian Sanders, Grover Rudolph, Kevin Thompson, Robert Jenkins, Jr. and Khari Reid, for joining me in the adventure that was jazzdigital Marketing.

To Chief Isha Mali Badjie for his spiritual guidance towards knowledge, wisdom and understanding.

To Marianne Williamson, whose inspiration and insights guided my first few tentative steps on my spiritual path.

To Dr. Marilyn French Hubbard, for her mentorship, partnership and friendship.

To Dr. William Pickard, for setting the example.

To Dr. Larry Gant. Without your support and flexibility, I could not have written this book at this time.

To Alicia Nails for making this book accessible with her editing and insight.

To Janice Jones for her committed listening.

To Landmark Education for providing the structure. Special thanks to Pat Reid Porter and Rosa Sims.

To Derek and Dawn Batts, Howard Bell, Rodgers Foster, Eleanor Josaitis, Domineca Neal, Rosa Sims, Sheila Washington, W. Bernard White and Mardi Woods whose stories contributed to the richness of this book.

To Laura Rodwan of Rodwan Communications, for her belief in me and in herself.

To Jambony Jarju, my personal companion on the spiritual path, my cousin and my friend.

To Charles L. Rencher, my love and my light, for teaching me, by example, about love every day.

To my ancestors, in deep gratitude for their assistance and support.

To the Creator. Thank you for all the blessings you have given me.

How To Use This Book

This book is intended to be a well-worn tool for your personal development. Use it actively—write on the pages and highlight the passages. It is a guide that will help you to engage yourself fully in the process of your spiritual growth.

From Fear to Faith is not specific to any religious affiliation. In this text, you will see more than one name for the Higher Power/God/Spirit/Creator that is the Source of us all. I use these names interchangeably and without a conscious preference.

I encourage you to find other seekers and to make your journey a fellowship in faith.

Despite its appearance, From Fear to Faith is not a static book—it is a dynamic creation that will be enhanced by your contributions, criticisms and insights. Please visit www.fromfeartofaith.com and dialogue with a community of entrepreneurs, each making their own steps on a common path.

Table of Contents

The spiritual path of the entrepreneur does not lead to a breakthrough where there is no fear – fear is always present. Fear coats the kernels of truth that we are not yet ready to digest. Behind our dark imaginings is the work of resolving ourselves to our experiences, our circumstances, our failures.

We will know fear throughout our lives. We can only hope to use it wisely. Fear is our signal to press forward toward the outer edges of our being and create something new – to be something new.

The power that we invoke in the process of that creation is faith.

The Beginning

I was facing the most challenging time of my career, trying to pull together the pieces of the small consulting firm that my business partner – my former professor and mentor – had begun and allowed me to run.

I came home late one night to his sobbing voice on my answering machine saying, "I didn't do it!"

That's how I found out that my business partner had been indicted and was facing rape and kidnapping charges. To my further shock and surprise, the case was the lead story on the local evening news. It turned out that the indictment had been handed down more than a year before. His former student and employee, a young woman he had earlier dismissed from another one of his businesses, was his accuser. This sensational case of "he said/she said" rocked our company. It was my job to hold the pieces together.

The reputation that we'd built up job by job, and the goodwill we used to generate new business had evaporated. Bills had to be paid and people had to be paid.

In the midst of the storm, I went to the most peaceful place I knew to clear my head. United Memorial Cemetery was where I could find the quiet comfort of my aunts and uncles and grandparents. Comfort, even when sepia-toned and delivered in faded whispers and memories, was what I really needed. As I sat in the cemetery, surrounded by my ancestors, I wondered how I got myself in this mess.

Sitting on the lush green grass, I heard a quiet voice in my head say the rather unlikely words that would start me on my path as an entrepreneur.

"Youth Entrepreneurship CD-ROM"

My favorite class in the MBA program at the University of Michigan was a simulation where a company's marketing decisions were entered into a computer and its stock prices were set based on those decisions. The insight I had received at the cemetery was, I was sure, a calling to create something similar as a way to dig out of the hole in which our company had found itself. I thought that maybe the youth entrepreneurship curriculum that our consulting firm had developed could be repackaged and sold as a computer game.

Later that same evening, as I joined a friend for a drink, I shared my plan for moving the business forward. Jokingly, I asked if she happened to know someone who could create the CD. To my surprise, she said that she had just met Vivian Sanders, a woman located not far from me in Detroit who could handle the job. I contacted her and set up a meeting.

A week later, while meeting with Vivian, I saw my future in a bright flash before my eyes. That future was a new company that would allow me to start fresh. The company that she and I were to start was called jazzdigital Marketing. From its inception, jazzdigital was a spiritual journey that challenged my intelligence, my patience, my perseverance and my sense of self. Born from struggle, ridiculously underfunded, and started in one of the worst recessions in recent years, jazzdigital was the perfect curriculum for teaching me about pride, hope, love, fear and faith.

Entrepreneurship

An entrepreneur is one who assumes personal risk and responsibility in the creation of an enterprise. The enterprise can be for-profit or non-profit, bootstrapped or well-funded, a franchise opportunity or an innovative upstart, a full-time occupation or a part-time hustle. According to the Kauffman Foundation, the creation of a new firm is more widespread in the United States than marriage or giving birth. Small businesses are the backbone of our economy and the lifeblood of our competitiveness; they are the stuff of the American Dream.

This Dream is attractive to entrepreneurs because of our tendency to believe that through hard work and force of will, we can create success. Entrepreneurs tend to believe they are "at cause" in any situation, and running a business is the perfect laboratory to test the theory.

There is a great opportunity when dynamic individuals meet dynamic situations – the opportunity for personal growth. Entrepreneurs grow as their businesses grow, and they grow even more as their businesses fail. From the dread that comes with having to lay off your staff, to the pride of realizing that your vision has generated the income for your employee to put her children through college, the implications of business ownership are powerful and meaningful, particularly because they are so tied with our personal identities.

The lenses through which we see ourselves in our businesses define us. Often we find comfort within that definition, whether it actually applies or not. Identity is "I" (or ourselves) in the context of our creations.

There is an even greater opportunity for growth for the entrepreneur – the opportunity for spiritual growth. As enlightened entrepreneurs, we can allow ourselves to have a different relationship with our worldly pursuits. The growth we experience also comes from allowing ourselves to be transformed in the process of achieving our business goals. It is less about doing and affecting our surroundings and more about who we are being in the face of our surroundings. That being colors our doing. The creative nature of entrepreneurship makes it much easier to be in the now, in the present, where being and doing co-exist. Participating in that creative process fully means allowing ourselves to evolve. Evolution is "I" in the context of our creativity.

This book follows the spiritual journey of the entrepreneur along a familiar path, from fear to faith. Fear and faith are a circle, marking the beginning and end, and beginning again, of spiritual evolution. There are events in our lives that give us the opportunity to either spiritually evolve or devolve. The first kiss on a date with someone with whom we can really connect – someone who sets the butterflies loose in our bellies – can trigger us to open ourselves to the possibility of love, or close our hearts in anticipation of the possibility of hurt. We choose fear or faith. Our first day at school or on the job can trigger emotions that, when brought down to their most basic component, are either fear or faith-driven.

Entrepreneurship brings with it the opportunity to see the dynamics of fear and faith in an up close and personal way. Successful entrepreneurs must *be* faith – and must generate faith for their employees, investors and customers. Without that most essential element, a company – especially one operating in hard times – cannot live up to its potential. In taking on the role of faith in action, entrepreneurs can be transformed. The enlightened entrepreneur can embrace that transformation as a source of power. From that power, other qualities are derived that contribute greatly to the growth of the individual and the company. Two of those qualities, drive and leadership, are keys to a way of being that brings about the extraordinary results required of successful business owners.

Drive

Drive is about being committed, sometimes in the face of enormous resistance to that commitment. It is a defining characteristic of successful entrepreneurs and a necessary survival skill.

I learned about drive from my mother and father. Both of them are driven, my mother in a less outwardly demonstrative way than my father, but driven nonetheless. Education is very important to them; they are both teachers. During my childhood, I received a solid academic foundation from some of the best schools available. My elementary and middle school years were spent in private schools, and then I attended Renaissance High School, a public school that is ranked as one of the best in the state. Unlike most public high schools in Detroit, entrance into Renaissance required the successful completion of an examination. Unfortunately, the test was only administered once a year, and I was scheduled to be out of the country on the day of the test.

My parents planned and paid for my month-long trip abroad many months in advance and did not want me to miss the opportunity. They also felt that since I had the grades and the desire, a simple calendar conflict should not stop me from attending my school of choice.

My mother sent letters to the school's administration, the assistant principal, the principal and anyone else at the school whose title she knew. As fellow teachers dedicated to excellence in education, she said, they should recognize the irony in not allowing her child into Renaissance. Her arguments fell on deaf ears, so she wrote every member of the Detroit Public School Board, as well as the superintendent. She argued that after paying decades of city taxes to fund public schools it did not make sense that her little girl should be denied a chance to attend a public school. The Board didn't listen.

My dad watched her stay up late, writing dozens of letters, making countless follow-up calls and bumping into a brick wall again and again. He decided that another form of drive might do the trick. He didn't shave for a few days and then took a day off from work. Wearing a dark blue skullcap pulled down low over his eyes, a black jogging suit, a dark blue pea coat, and an attitude straight out of *Shaft*, he showed up at the superintendent's office and announced that he wasn't going to leave until he talked to the superintendent and straightened the matter out. He made his point. A few weeks later, I took the test in a special session administered by Detroit Public Schools staff. I only missed one question and was admitted in the fall of 1983.

I learned a lot from that incident. I learned that it sometimes takes an unconventional path to achieve a result. I also learned that you cannot stop at someone else's "no." There is a great deal of power in personally demonstrating a commitment to a particular stand. My father's tactics might not be as successful today as they were in 1983. In a post-September 11th world, he might have been stopped at the door, thrown in jail, or worse. But he showed up and took a stand. That made the difference.

Drive As Persistence

There are times when, as an entrepreneur, persistence is the key. You work diligently to bring an employee over the learning curve. You convince an important potential client with presentation after presentation, and proposal after proposal, that you will increase their bottom line. You fill out the paperwork with the bank. You go your rounds with the IRS. You persist and you persevere. You grow. Patience becomes a part of who you are. You synchronize yourself to the pace of what is, you catch your breath and you begin to understand a key aspect of faith.

You get to know time as a subjective thing, a learning tool that goes as fast or as slow as needed to learn the lesson. Drive as persistence becomes less about effort and more about an extension of commitment to a result. The spiritual growth inherent in that state of being makes it possible to move mountains. It is the quiet power that Gandhi wielded, and this power is what sustains a company over the long haul.

Drive As Force

There are times when entrepreneurs must express their drive as force. You face down a competitor threatening to overtake your territory. You confront a dishonest employee. You deal with missed delivery dates. You negotiate pricing with your vendors. You resolve issues with your landlord. You build confidence and strength and the reputation that comes from exuding those qualities.

Drive as force wells up in front of you, affecting circumstances even before you step into them. It trails behind you, leaving a lasting impression. This type of spiritual growth makes it possible to be a magnified version of your ordinary self. It is Malcolm X's smoldering "by any means necessary" intensity. Using that power keeps the barbarians from crashing the gate, and it puts them down if they make it inside.

Leadership

Leadership, the second key quality for the enlightened entrepreneur, is at the heart of what it is to be an entrepreneur. It is part and parcel of most entrepreneurs' personalities and helps them to define themselves within their companies. Leadership is the difference between employer and employee, because most people either don't have the necessary vision or are unwilling to accept bottom-line accountability for a business.

jazzdigital Marketing was the epitome of a business with maximal vision and minimal accountability. We had major dreams about changing the way urban communities interacted, but never developed a game plan with clearly defined responsibilities that could get us there. We conceptualized a host of products, but never followed through with developing them for the marketplace. As the president and CEO of the company, I often wondered how such smart people could make such a small amount of money. The bottom line was that the extraordinary results were lacking because my leadership did not include accountability.

Accountability without vision can also stifle growth. Most of us know of small companies that are going to stay small because they lack vision. They focus themselves on the art of perfecting their businesses within a certain comfort level.

When accountability and vision are in balance, leaders can achieve the extraordinary. Eleanor Josaitis is an example of a leader who has successfully maintained that balance. Ms. Josaitis is co-founder (along with the late Catholic priest, Father William Cunningham) and the former CEO of Focus: HOPE, a community-based organization founded in 1968, after the Detroit riots. Their mission is simple and profoundly inspirational:

Recognizing the dignity and beauty of every person, we pledge intelligent and practical action to overcome racism, poverty and injustice. And to build a metropolitan community where all people may live in freedom, harmony, trust and affection. Black and white, yellow, brown and red from Detroit and its suburbs, of every economic status, national origin and religious persuasion we join in this covenant.

Focus: HOPE has redefined social entrepreneurship by expanding its capabilities from providing traditional social assistance services to fashioning itself as a competitive, ISO 9001-certified supplier to the automotive industry. In 2003, the organization generated more than $34 million in production revenue. Josaitis says:

Father Cunningham and I were a very good team because we would debate and argue about everything and that builds your creative juices. We knew that because we were catching so much flack, we had to be accountable for everything we did and that was just the mindset that we started with.

The vision was always "bring communities together" and I tell you from the bottom of my heart, the mission statement is what drove us all these years. Intelligent and practical action, and that's what we kept saying. "It's got to be intelligent. It's got to be practical but it's

got to be some action." We just didn't want to talk
about it; we wanted action.

The Path

Entrepreneurship can be an intensely personal, almost
messianic enterprise. There is a higher calling, mission
or vision that often drives the business owner to work
at an unreasonable pace toward their goal. Fourteen-
hour days, a lack of interest in leisurely pursuits and
unwavering focus on business are characteristics of
many entrepreneurs that cause others to scratch their
heads in wonderment.

We are modern-day monks, with an otherworldly
zeal centered on a worldly calling. The opportunity to
expand the experience and discover a spiritual context
within the world of business ownership is available to
those who seek it. The spiritual path of the
entrepreneur is a gift that allows us to provide a
positive meaning to the experiences we have on the
entrepreneurial journey. Our successes will be defined
not by our possessions, but by the happiness and
fulfillment we experience and share with others.
Ultimately, the spiritual path is a tool that allows us to
give relevance to our lives, ourselves and the world.

The usefulness of a cup is in its emptiness

Chinese proverb

Fear

is a question:

What are you afraid of, and why?

Just as the seed of health is in illness, because illness contains information, your fears are a treasure house of self-knowledge if you explore them.

Marilyn Ferguson

Meditation

The mass of men lead lives of quiet desperation.
What is called resignation is confirmed desperation.

Henry David Thoreau

Questions to consider

1 What are your biggest and most persistent complaints concerning your life?

2 What would life look like if you took a dramatic step forward in those areas of your life that you complain about?

4 How much responsibility do you take for not having what you want in your life?

3 Who or what do you think is stopping you from taking those steps?

5 What do you notice about the conversation you had with yourself when answering the questions above?

Step 1:
Overcome Inertia

How many people do you know who are perpetually planning to start a business? Most people know at least one person who has gone beyond the usual baseline business planning and ventured off into the land of "analysis paralysis." They have met with potential business partners and discussed potential revenues, prospected potential clients, scrutinized potential pitfalls and dreamt about potential profits, all with little emphasis on how to turn that potential into reality. They are much more comfortable with the idea of entrepreneurship than with actually being an entrepreneur, and with good reason. Entrepreneurship is a scary concept. Most people are resigned to stand on the sidelines of entrepreneurship; few are willing to play such a (sometimes) brutal game.

If you are one of those paralyzed people, you know about the fear that comes with hanging out your shingle. The idea of failure is a direct threat to the ego, and, as humans, placating our egos is one of the highest priorities of our unconscious minds.

Comforting our egos leads to the downward spiral of procrastination and the endless cycle of "placebo planning." Our launch dates are pushed back and our job situations seem a bit more bearable. Our fear, disguised as prudence, pulls the strings in the background, and we get lulled into a puppet's existence. We end up living lives of "quiet desperation," afraid to cut ourselves free of the rote and the routine.

Three Persistent Excuses

As potential entrepreneurs, we allow our fear to create the excuses that we tell ourselves in order to justify not following through on our business ideas. There are three excuses in particular that chime the loudest. "It takes too much time!" "It takes too much money!" "I don't know enough." Each of these reasons can be valid today, but they do not have to be valid tomorrow. Taking a look at each one of these excuses individually will give us some insight on how to move past them.

It Takes Too Much Time!

In most people's perception, time is something that is strictly measured and allocated, and usually the allocation is not enough. It can feel like the yardstick Sister Stella wielded in your eighth grade mathematics class – cold, unyielding, and ruthless. In reality, time is a man-made concept that man then forgot he made. Time can bend to our experiences. When we are in love, time becomes elasticized, like salt-water taffy. It stretches out a single moment – a touch, a kiss – into eternity.

When we are involved in activities that we are passionate about, time can have that same rubber quality. Consider that time is something we make, not something we have. Once you make the conscious choice to put time and effort into your enterprise, time can often be your ally. You are able to take an eight-hour day and produce at a much higher rate than you would working for someone else. The resistance that shows up on a job you don't enjoy no longer holds you back. You free yourself by focusing on the bliss of your enterprise, and time expands to accommodate your dreams.

It Takes Too Much Money!

Our relationship with money is similar to our relationship with time. Money is a man-made concept that we have each infused with our own meaning. Poverty can be a righteous state for some, or a reason to commit suicide for others. The presence of money, even as an intangible blip on a computer screen, makes us feel secure — even when there is no guarantee that the blip won't be erased. A quick flash of money at the casino or on TV quickens our pulses and heightens our senses. Billboard ads announcing the size of the lottery jackpot makes us stare off into space and think about how problem-free our lives would be if we could just get some m-o-n-e-y.

The reality is that money by itself has no intrinsic value; it is a blank canvas upon which we express our prejudices, our fantasies, our desires and our fears.

Our conscious and unconscious emotional and psychological projections about money contribute to our tendency to attract it or repel it. The idea that it takes too much money to pursue our entrepreneurial dreams is more often a programmed "pledge of allegiance" to the idea of scarcity than it is a carefully-researched assessment. Our vow of scarcity makes us project thoughts that the amount of money we have is and always will be less than we want, or in some cases, need. Often, we do not even determine just what it would take to accomplish what we want to do. We just assume that we don't have it and we never will. We tell ourselves that abundance and free-flowing money are for other folks – those impossibly rich, beautiful people we see on TV.

Interestingly enough, once we start relating to money as simply something that we have or don't have at this moment – without projecting a future that is based heavily on this current state – it becomes much easier to control the flow of this asset. This gives us access to the dynamic creation of money and frees us from assumptions of a rote extension of the past. You see the same principle at work with people who are not negatively invested in their weight. They are able to lose or gain at will, rather than constantly complaining without actually taking any action. Discovering your beliefs about money brings about a powerful opportunity for spiritual growth.

I Don't Know Enough!

One of the best excuses for not starting a business an excessive focus on is not knowing enough. Indeed, if you are an accomplished pastry chef trying to break into the aerospace industry, the validity of "I don't know enough" is glaring. One of the most important things that lenders and potential partners and customers look for in a business owner is expertise and experience specific to the target industry. Most people who are interested in starting a business are not pastry chefs trying to start up the next Boeing. They are people who have a skill that they use every day, or a familiar hobby they truly enjoy, or some pursuit with a short learning curve and they decide to make a go of it. Technical expertise is rarely the issue.

There are at least two underlying assumptions behind the "not knowing enough" excuse.

1. It is possible to ever "know enough."
2. Knowing enough will keep a business from failing.

Entrepreneurs know that "knowing enough" is a fallacy, and there is always more to learn. The mechanics of a business, from an employee's point of view—even a manager's point of view—are quite different from that of an owner. There are whole new dimensions to consider. Total accountability for all functions of the business begins and ends with the owner. There are certain aspects of the business that can be delegated or outsourced, but the ultimate responsibility rests squarely on the owner's shoulders.

Entrepreneurs also know that success is never, ever guaranteed. Established corporations with decades of business history and thousands of brilliant minds have failed spectacularly, and will continue to do so. Small business owners are at least as vulnerable as Kmart or Worldcom. Actually, for entrepreneurs, failure is not just a possibility; it is a probability. Risk is an inherent part of small business ownership. Knowledge can only mitigate that risk, it cannot eliminate it.

According to W. Bernard White, founder of White Construction, a multimillion dollar firm started in 1989, business start up begins with a gut check.

When I went into business, I had absolutely no projects in hand. I had prospects at best. I tell folk I just had the balls to do it. I was crazy enough to try it. I understood that if it didn't work for me, I could always find another job, which was all I had anyway.

In an almost paradoxical way, there is a very special opportunity in "I don't know enough." There are times when looking for a preconceived outcome obscures the emergence of a better result. You have heard of instances where people did not know enough to realize they were doing the impossible. The constraints that we allow our past experiences and patterns to put on our success can hobble us before we are out of the gate.

The power of "I don't know enough" is embodied in the concept of the beginner's mind. The beginner's mind is the mind without preconceptions and expectations, judgments and prejudices. The beginner's mind is firmly located in the present, to explore and observe things as they are truly are right now. Interacting with your surroundings, using your beginner's mind, allows you a level of freedom and creativity that can lead to remarkable results. As Zen master Shunryu

Suzuki eloquently stated, "In the beginner's mind there are many possibilities. In the expert's mind there are few."

Rosa Sims, an organizational development consultant, trainer/facilitator and productivity coach relates an interesting story about not knowing.

One of the first things I remember saying to a client is, "I don't have the answer, but I've got some tools and we can grapple with it together."

I was scared to death to say that. I mean, this was my first paying client. If I tell them that I don't have the answer, I might lose the contract. I can't afford to lose this contract – it's the only one I've got, if I've got it, but I don't know if I've even got it. I don't know the answer and I'd be bullshitting them if I kept sitting here trying to figure out something so I'm just going to tell them.

My client looked at me and she says, "You know what, I didn't expect you to have the answer. What I really need is someone to work with me to get to whatever it is that needs to be done and if you're willing to work with me, then you have the job."

I became comfortable with saying I don't know, which was a major step for me. I think that's probably been refreshing for my clients. Saying I don't know actually creates a space where we can create something, as opposed to, I've got this cookie-cutter answer because there is no 'one size fits all.'"

Once released from these largely illusory fears, you need never again waste time and energy trying to fix your weaknesses. You will have freed yourself to exploit your strengths fully. This singular ability is what separates the outrageously successful business owner from the rest of the pack.

Toolkit

Examining the excuses you make about starting your business means facing your fears about your business. Use the questions below to gain insight into your fears. Learn how they impact your ability to create an empowered future for yourself.

Fears	Questions to Ask
I don't have enough time.	1. What are you committed to? What is your priority? 2. How much time do you spend on things that you are committed to? 3. How much time do you spend on things that you are not committed to? 4. How much time are you willing to devote to starting your business?
I don't have enough money.	1. Do you know how much money it will take to start your business? 2. How much do you (and your family) spend every month? 3. Where do you spend your money? 4. What non-monetary resources can you access that will help you start your business?
I don't know enough	1. What information do you need to start your business? 2. If your life depended on having that information within the next two weeks, where could you get it? 3. What three things are most likely to cause your business to fail? 4. What qualities or traits do you lack that you believe would increase the likelihood of your business success?

Draw Your Disaster

Imagine the most disastrous outcome of your entrepreneurial efforts that you can envision. Now detail, describe and draw that disaster. Face your biggest fear. For an extra bonus, share your drawing with someone supportive.

Homework

Meditation

Self-trust is the first secret of success.

Ralph Waldo Emerson

Men succeed when they realize that their failures are the preparation for their victories.

Ralph Waldo Emerson

Questions to consider

1 What was your greatest personal failure?

2 What impact did it have on your life?

3 Which personal failure has taught you the most?

4 What did it teach you?

5 If you knew you could not fail, would you do things differently?

Step 2: Embrace the Gift of Failure

The vast majority of entrepreneurs will experience some form of failure. Small failures can occur during the day-to-day management of business. Large failures can take entrepreneurs completely out of the game.

Failure is more than a word – it is also a conceptual mind trap that can incapacitate even the most enthusiastic of entrepreneurs. There is a "failure mind trap" that triggers the deepest, darkest fears and doubts and hobbles the entrepreneur's confidence.

Characteristics of the Failure Mind Trap

One of the characteristics of the failure mind trap that makes it so frightening is that it is highly subjective. One person's complete malfunction can be another's minor hiccup. The failure mind trap is therefore a customized construct, tailored to an individual's unique experiences and fears. Imagination feeds it, just as effectively as it feeds an individual's concept of success.

Another aspect of the failure mind trap that makes it so powerful is that its core is composed of the power we have given to our idea of failure – not from failure itself. We can make our business failures mean that we are personally inadequate. What's worse, we can utterly confuse this subjective internalization with objective facts that we pick and choose to justify our failure mind trap.

The failure mind trap is also deeply personal. Failure is not only popularly defined as "the condition or fact of not achieving the desired end or ends", but also as "one who fails". Within the failure mind trap, the failure experience and the person experiencing the failure are so tightly associated that it is difficult to ascertain where one ends and the other begins.

Examining Failure

When you and God are aligned in the statement, "Let there be…", whatever is to be created at the end of that statement will undoubtedly be manifested.

When there is a conflict, it means that you simply cannot see the success that has been created by God for you in the present moment. We can use any number of models to analyze the conventional causes for business failure; however, there is another level of analysis – a spiritual level – that can truly be illuminating. The root of the spiritual analysis of our failures is recognizing the opportunity that exists in failure. Creation breaks down when we are not aligned with Spirit, either through lack of faith or lack of integrity. Lack of faith shuts down our ability to perceive God's creative force working in our lives. Lack of integrity is our inability to make our word into reality.

It is important to note that the only source of conflict can be your perception of God's creative force and your ability to generate your own creative force. God always creates for you. Spirit may create something incredible in your life that is for your greatest good, even if you cannot see it. This is where the examination of faith and integrity become critically important.

Ask yourself the following questions to help you align your faith and integrity. Make your responses as honest and thorough as possible and notice any resistance you have to the questions.

Faith: What structure do I have to strengthen my faith? How do I communicate with my Creator and how does my Creator communicate with me? Communion with Spirit can take many forms – through words, song, painting, dance, meditation. Which form resonates with you? How do you work through lapses in faith? What fellowship have you created to bolster your faith? What conversations are you having about faith that keeps it real and alive both in your heart and in your mind?

Integrity: Can you be counted on to do what you say you will do? Who are you accountable to for your words? Can you be criticized? Have you invited people in your life to hear your promises and your dreams and to hold you to them? What is your typical response to being late, to being caught in a lie, or to being caught not doing what you said you were going to do? Do you justify your action or inaction? Do you ignore it and hope others will as well? Do you get angry or seek sympathy? Can you identify your weaknesses, both in business and in life? Are you afraid to know what they are?

Answering these questions is a critical step on the spiritual path of the entrepreneur. Failure, for the enlightened entrepreneur, is a powerful tool. Its power is directly correlated to the lesson that we are willing to learn from it.

Domineca Neal is a corporate marketing whiz turned serial entrepreneur who has experienced both success and failure in business ownership.

In my personal experience, faith was really key during my most recent business opportunity, when my partner and I started having issues in the partnership. There were times when money was being drained out of the company and I could not control the situation because we were 50-50 partners. Near the end, I remember managing the company's cash flow and regardless of the [accounting and financial] skills I brought to the table, a key element was praying we would reach a resolution or that something would happen that would allow me to perform the tasks needed to keep the business running.

A partnership is very similar to marriage. Finding myself in a unfavorable partnership was painful, because I was in a situation where I had to interact with this person and things were deplorable. It was faith that allowed me to get through each day, day by day, in the hope that there would be resolution. You're working so hard in the business, you're giving it 200%, and to have something you can't fix, it tore me down. I think it was faith that allowed me to get through and have peace of mind and focus on a solution instead of having a lot of other emotions come into play and drive the process.

Seven Lessons of Failure

Below are seven ways in which business failure can provide us with some of the best lessons that entrepreneurship has to offer.

1. **Failure reminds us that we are assuming risk.** Sometimes, especially while experiencing financial

success based on decisions made with our business instincts rather than sound justifications, we can lose sight of the fact that we have "skin in the game." We forget that business ownership is a risky enterprise and that the business deserves to be run with some degree of accountability. When we experience failure we remember that the discipline required to justify our actions with research and due diligence is often well worth the time it takes.

2. **Failure makes us realize how many people depend on our success.** As entrepreneurs, we sometimes get caught up in the idea that we bear all the risk of the enterprise. Failure reminds us that our employees, our vendors, our creditors and our families all depend on our success. There are many employees who forgo greater salaries and greater perks at other companies in order to work with a small company because they believe in the founder's vision. When a company fails, it can ripple into layoffs at the coffee shop on the corner and bankruptcies with key vendors. Not making the third quarter numbers, even in an unfavorable environment, can mean that the entire sales team has to work overtime to make up the difference, resulting in a drop in quality time with their families. Failure, both big and small, reminds us that our own futures and fortunes aren't the only ones at risk.

3. **Failure teaches us that maintenance is important.** Entrepreneurship allows us to be visionary, to entertain the Big Ideas. Unfortunately, it is difficult to maintain the energy and excitement of the Big Idea from its conception to its implementation and ongoing operation. Maintenance is boring, unsexy work. But success is a marathon, not a sprint. It is not about the panache with which you can bring new ideas to market, it is about how you monitor and manage their growth and maturation. Failure can expose our distain for the minutiae managers —and reveal our dependence on them.

4. **Failure promotes systems-based thinking.** After all the fingers have been pointed, failure can teach us that it wasn't about the people —the processes may not work. It is much easier to lay blame on a person than to critically examine a business model that a company has grown dependent upon, but failure gives us the opportunity to do just that. An entrepreneur who takes the time to question fundamental assumptions can move from reaction to proaction and avert a catastrophe.

5. **Failure gives us the chance to learn something new.** Sometimes failure comes as a result of not staying ahead of the learning curve. In order to stave off competition, we must know about new technological,

regulatory, economic and societal trends. To beat the competition, we must be able to predict these trends before they appear. We have to commit to being life-long learners and to invest the time and money necessary to support the market position we desire. Putting out the everyday fires can distract us from that commitment. Failure reminds us that without forward thinking, we can be win the battle but lose the war.

6. **Failure helps us to refocus.** Devastating failures allow us to realign our priorities. Closing a company can be incredibly traumatic, but this type of trial can help us to develop an appreciation for the support of our friends. We can examine the hours we devoted to the business and compare them to the amount of quality time we spent with our families. We can also check our spiritual barometer and find out if we adhered to the values and ethics that we espouse outside the business.

7. **Failure helps us to become better entrepreneurs.** Failure is a natural part of the adaptive process of entrepreneurship. It goes hand in hand with innovation. Without failure and innovation, there is complacency and inertia, leaving your company vulnerable to someone unafraid to be bold. Failure tests and toughens us. It is an integral part of the spiritual path because it turns our focus away from our distant desti-

nation of success and allows us to consider the path we must take to get there.

Choosing failure as our teacher allows us to access the power of commitment. Domineca Neal can testify to the positive aspects of embracing failure.

You think you know who you are and what your values are, says Neal. Your faith is tested when you are at your lowest point and I would say that's when your values are tested, too.

When things were really tough, that's when I saw who I was and I liked who I was, that was a good feeling. Even at my lowest point, I did the right thing. Before, when I had said that integrity was always important to me, I had never been really tested. I was actually tested and I'm glad I was who I thought I was. I passed the test.

Toolkit

The key to escaping the failure mind trap is to get it out of your head (where it is aided by your imagination) and to separate the concept of failure from the experiences, feelings and meaning you have associated with failing. Perform a cold, clinical analysis of failure. Define it. Determine its causes. Do the forensics and get the facts–especially if you have actually experienced the failure instead of just anticipating it. Were you under-capitalized? How was your cash flow? Did the team have the appropriate skill set for the business? These are the types of questions that begin the process.

The spiritual path of the entrepreneur involves an advanced level of thinking. Use the grid below to gain insight about your three biggest business failures from a business perspective and from a spiritual perspective.

Failure	Business Analysis	Spiritual Analysis

Escape the Trap

Take the time to complete the grid as thoroughly as you can. Be prepared to share your work with someone supportive.

Homework

Meditation

Our deepest fear is not that we are inadequate. Our deepest fear is that we are powerful beyond measure. It is our light, not our darkness, that most frightens us. We ask ourselves, who am I to be brilliant, gorgeous, talented and fabulous? Actually, who are you not to be? You are a child of God. Your playing small does not serve the world. There is nothing enlightened about shrinking so that other people won't feel insecure about you. We were born to manifest the glory of God that is within us. It's not just in some of us; it's in everyone. And as we let our own light shine, we unconsciously give other people permission to do the same. As we are liberated from our own fear, our presence automatically liberates others.

Marianne Williamson

Questions to consider

1 In what areas of your life do you feel inadequate?

2 What past events have led you to develop feelings of inadequacy?

3 What kinds of challenges trigger your feelings of inadequacy?

4 What dreams have you deferred, based on your feelings of inadequacy?

5 What do you notice about the conversation you had with yourself when answering the questions above?

Step 3: Examine Your Inadequacy

Feelings of inadequacy create a consistent background context for entrepreneurs, whether they are consciously aware of them or not. It is the other shoe dropping, the failure we dread. It is the fuel that drives the "never let 'em see you sweat" shield that we create to protect us from showing signs of weakness or self-doubt. We don't want vendors, partners, or customers to sense our feelings of personal lack.

Why do we work so hard against our feelings of inadequacy, especially when we know that, at some point in their lives, everyone has them? It is, in part, because we are in the habit of projecting ourselves as high-powered, aggressive, take-charge leaders in whom people can place their trust. We also stifle feelings of inadequacy to insulate ourselves from the criticisms of others. We know that most people are not willing to make the bottom-line decision and be responsible for results because they feel inadequate themselves. Our employees, friends and associates are much more comfortable talking about what they would do if they were in our position than daring to follow their own dreams.

The bravado and arrogance required to be an entrepreneur also makes us unwilling to face up to our feelings of inadequacy. We see ourselves as extraordinary visionaries, not limited by the mental traps that catch ordinary people. We have the arrogance to believe that we can succeed where others have failed or feared to tread. Inadequacy and arrogance are opposite sides of the same coin. One is always in the background of the other.

The bottom line is that we resist our feelings of inadequacy because we do not value them. We cannot see any worth in the phrase, "I am not enough." Giving that phrase room to breathe in our minds is like Superman holding on to kryptonite. There is, however, another possibility. It is entirely possible that those feelings of inadequacy are a gift. For many entrepreneurs, the idea that feeling personally insufficient is a good thing is an unfathomable thought. It runs counter to the core of our identities as entrepreneurs.

Consultant Rosa Sims remembers feeling she had to know all the answers.

I was used to knowing – all the time. I knew the answer before you opened your mouth. I knew the answer maybe even before you asked the question and if I didn't know the answer, I'm not going to open my mouth and say 'I don't know' because I might look stupid.

Acknowledging our feelings of inadequacy is a gift because it frees us to focus on moving forward, to learn the necessary lessons and to go to the next step.

Examining Inadequacy

Feelings of inadequacy are permanent. No matter how much success we have in our businesses and in our lives, feelings of inadequacy will lurk in the background.

Mardi Woods, marketing consultant and National Vice President for Warm Spirit gave her thoughts about how inadequacy can hold us back from our breakthroughs.

I can recall working with one of our consultants who was pressing forward to promote to becoming an executive in Warm Spirit, a network marketing health and beauty products company targeting (but not limited to) African American women. We were discussing what was preventing her breakthrough.

I asked her about what was her personal daily affirmation and she responded, "I have a good life." We agreed that she did in fact have a good life and had a lot to be grateful for, but that it was that same gratefulness that was holding her back – preventing her from feeling that she deserved more. I related well to her because I too shared her obstacle – how dare we ask for more.

Even after achieving some level of success you have to continue to strive for more and believe that you deserve it or you will become stagnated. Your fear of moving past where you believe you should be must be conquered. My advice is to move past that fear by staying grounded in your purpose, in what moving to the next level can do for you, your family, and your community.

If we really look at ourselves, inadequacy shows up in some measure in the decisions we make about the car we drive, the relationships we create and the way we run our businesses.

There is a practical purpose to considering the possibility of inadequacy as a gift. Valuing inadequacy helps us to stop resisting its permanence. Rather than driving our decisions in the background, inadequacy can be brought out of the subconscious into the conscious realm. Facing and embracing our feelings of inadequacy frees us to give those feelings meaning that works for us. Let's consider the gift of inadequacy.

Background and Crisis Inadequacy

Inadequacy exists in the spaces between our victories. It is an indistinct construct that, left unexamined, can escape our recognition and even our awareness. The first step in receiving inadequacy as a gift is gaining the ability to distinguish it and its impact on our lives. Inadequacy is defined as "Not adequate; unequal to the purpose; insufficient; deficient; not meeting the requirements especially of a task." There are two forms of inadequacy: background inadequacy and crisis inadequacy.

Background inadequacy creates the context of many of our subconscious decisions. It is passive, pervasive and potent. Background inadequacy is what advertisers play on to sell us our cars, our perfumes and our clothes. It is particularly powerful for entrepreneurs, who often possess an innate need for some level of acclaim or recognition.

Crisis inadequacy is the fear that rises in a challenging moment to grip us by the throat. It is active, confrontational and powerful. It is the risk that fuels the adrenaline rush of entrepreneurship. It is the authoritative voice from within that says, "I am not enough." Entrepreneurs often confront crisis inadequacy because we so often confront crises.

The Purpose of Inadequacy

The feeling of inadequacy arises within us for a special purpose. Its gift is that it reminds us that we cannot do what we were meant to do on this earth by ourselves. The terror that we feel as we attempt some new challenge or face some old fear is not a signal to stop. It is a signal to move forward hand in hand with our Creator. It is a built-in mechanism that alerts us to the need to connect with our higher Self so that we can go forth in confidence. Recognizing that we have goals beyond our ability to fulfill them frees us to seek that which fills in the gap.

Howard Bell, five-time entrepreneur and president of a Detroit-based startup educational firm, discusses how business ownership can stretch your capabilities and expose feelings of inadequacy.

You get into entrepreneurship and you realize that it calls on all your business skills. I used to always pride myself on the fact that I never had to sell. I've been an engineer. I've been a lawyer. Those where just places where you can just walk in and you just basically worked. You had a task and you have to complete it. I said I was never going to be a salesman. I felt like it was sucking up. I just felt like it was a place I didn't want to be.

Then all of a sudden, you get into entrepreneurship and selling is like a regular part of your day. If you're not selling, you're not in entrepreneurship. Whether you're selling your company or you're selling your own abilities or you're selling a product, you are always selling. So for me, there was a weakness I had to overcome.

My thing about entrepreneurship is if you have a weakness, it'll get exposed. You'll have to work on it. You'll have to figure out how to either get somebody to help you with it or get better on your own (or try to avoid it as much as you can).

Becoming clear about our background inadequacy helps to reinforce the habit of connection. We need to be consistently prayerful and meditative to really examine ourselves and the motivation behind our decisions. Success is a function of our ability to maintain an ongoing spiritual connection that we can translate into purposeful action. A heightened sense of our background inadequacy can motivate us to create a spiritual structure that goes beyond habit and truly sustains us.

Crisis inadequacy is our Creator saying, "Let Me help you!" It is our access to a transformed state in which Spirit is in control. We can only receive this gift when we are able to relax, "let go and let God." It does not mean that we should stop doing that which needs to be done, it just means that we need to recognize that God has already taken the reins and we should not get in the way. We get in the way when we produce an excessive amount of worry, stress and drama. It is as ridiculous and purposeless as a child being afraid that she is about to fall when her mother has her securely in her hands. Once we stop the theatrics, we can see that everything is in divine order. Crisis inadequacy gives us the opportunity to trust in things unseen. It is an access to walking by faith, acting in flow and living in the *dunamis*, or the power, of God.

Dawn Batts is a longtime entrepreneur, currently working as chief operating officer of Union Heritage Capital Management, a financial management company with institutional clients that was founded by her husband, Derek Batts. She is also a pet supply store franchisee. She describes the moment she became an entrepreneur as a natural flow of divine order.

> *I remember when it first hit me that I should be on my own. I literally cried because it literally hit me. It was almost like spiritually within, [a voice said] 'It's time to go.'*
>
> *I thought, "What am I going to do?" I did not have the first contract, had not written a business plan. All the things you're taught in business school I had not completed, and yet I told other people this is what they should do.*
>
> *It was clear, spiritually, that it was time to go. I had been in prayer and in deep Bible study, probably about*

four or five months at that point. So it was very clear that it was time to go. So I made that decision.

The phrase "I am not enough" can actually be a comforting thought. Understanding that you can have what you want because you will not be alone in achieving it helps to alleviate the stress and strain of the Superman/Superwoman burden that entrepreneurs often place on themselves. The unshakable confidence that comes from this comfort is not positive thinking; it is positive knowing.

Toolkit

Unexamined feelings of inadequacy can create an impact on our lives without us even being aware of their effects. Use the table on page 60 to critically review some of the areas of your business.

There are five core areas of management for entrepreneurs. Below are some compelling thoughts that reveal opportunities for action in each area.

1. Managing People. One of the biggest challenges for entrepreneurs is to just let go. Let go of the attitude that you must have hands-on control of all aspects of your business. Let go of the belief that only you can make decisions. Delegate. Allow people to have the responsibility and authority they need to have to do their jobs. Ask yourself if the team that started the company can manage its growth. If not, make a change. Don't lower your standards for loyalty's sake. Ensure that the right people are in position and let them contribute. If you do not, your business will ultimately fail.

2. Managing Operations. It is dangerous to assume that what you have done in the past will always work. Prepare yourself for change by building performance indicators into your operations that allow you to monitor your performance. Check those measurements on a regular basis. Develop specific and objective procedures to identify and deal with problems. Doing things the same way, despite new market demands and changing times, exposes your company to unacceptable risk. Track your competition's movements. Educate yourself about the latest technologies that are relevant to your business. Be open to new ideas and technologies whose relevance has not yet been proven. Experiment.

3. Managing Products and Services. Is your product or service seasonal or volatile? What are the parameters for quality as defined by your customers? Determine what your customer needs, then find every way possible to give it to them. Recognize that purchasing and using your product is a total experience – don't just focus on the basic product itself.

4. Managing Perceptions. Who are your customers? You should be able to clearly identify them in one or two sentences. How are you going to reach them? How loyal are your potential customers to their current supplier? Do customers keep coming back or do they only purchase from you one time? Does it take a long time to close a sale or are your customers more driven by impulse buying? How do they perceive you? How do you want them to perceive you?

5. Managing Cash Flow. Sales activity does not necessarily equal a positive bottom line. You need to have enough cash to carry you until your business becomes profitable – so you need to be able to accurately predict how long that will be. Consider both business and personal living expenses when determining how much cash

Toolkit (continued)

you will need. You must also clearly define your pricing strategy. Is your product priced at a premium or at a value? Are you able to secure a lower cost than your competition? How are you managing your debt?

Area	Background Inadequacy	Crisis Inadequacy
People Management		
Cash Flow Management		
Operations Management		
Perceptions Management		
Product Management		

Stop Punishing Yourself

Keep a journal of all you anti-affirmative thoughts and words for the next 48 hours. Pay particular attention to the anti-affirmations that occur while you are working.

	Anti-Affirmation	Summary of Situation
Morning		
Afternoon		
Evening		
Morning		
Afternoon		
Evening		

Homework

Meditation

And he said unto them, "Within each of us lies the
power of our consent to health and to sickness,
to riches and to poverty, to freedom and to slavery.
It is we who control these, and not another."

A mill-man spoke and said, "Easy words for you,
Master, for you are guided as we are not,
and need not toil as we toil. A man has
to work for his living in this world."

The Master answered and said,
"Once there lived a village of creatures along the
bottom of a great crystal river.

The current of the river swept silently
over them all -- young and old, rich and poor,
good and evil, the current going its own way,
knowing only its own crystal self.

Each creature in its own manner clung tightly to the
twigs and rocks of the river bottom, for clinging
was their way of life, and resisting the current
was what each had learned from birth.

But one creature said at last, 'I am tired of clinging.
Though I cannot see it with my eyes, I trust that the
current knows where it is going.
I shall let go, and let it take me where it will.
Clinging, I shall die of boredom.' The other
creatures laughed and said, 'Fool! Let go, and that
current you worship will throw you tumbled
and smashed across the rocks,
and you will die quicker than boredom!'

But the one heeded them not, and taking a breath
did let go, and at once was tumbled and smashed
by the current across the rocks.

Yet in time, as the creature refused to cling again,
the current lifted him free from the bottom,
and he was bruised and hurt no more.

And the creatures downstream, to whom
he was a stranger, cried, 'See a miracle!
A creature like ourselves, yet he flies!
See the Messiah, come to save us all!'

And the one carried in the current said, 'I am no
more Messiah than you. The river delights
to lift us free, if only we dare to let go.
Our true work is this voyage, this adventure.'

"But they cried the more, 'Saviour!' all while
clinging to the rocks, and when they looked again
he was gone, and they were left alone making
legends of a Saviour."

Richard Bach

Questions
to consider

1 What beliefs are you clinging to?

2 Who in your life encourages your entrepreneurial efforts?

3 Who in your life discourages your entrepreneurial efforts?

4 How many people do you know who live out their entrepreneurial dreams vicariously through you?

5 What do you notice about the conversation you had with yourself when answering the questions above?

Step 4:
Forgive
the Fearful

Every entrepreneur feels pressure from people inside their business world. Customers, employees, vendors and other direct stakeholders all have competing demands that make the juggling act of business ownership that much more difficult and exciting. The tension created from so many differing agendas is part of what makes the entrepreneurial environment so intense. It is a dynamic that is an inherent part of owning a business.

Alongside most entrepreneurs' business existence is their personal existence. Unlike with many other professions, entrepreneurs can experience a great deal of conflict from indirect stakeholders – usually family and friends – about their business choices (or more specifically, their choice to be in business for themselves).

Eleanor Josaitis, co-founder of Focus: HOPE, faced a lot of resistance from her family in the late 1960s when she, a white, suburbanite housewife, took an active role in combating the racial tension that led to and followed the Detroit riots.

When the riots hit, we walked the streets the day of the riots and we said we've got to do something. [Father Cunningham] quit his teaching profession, took the Madonna parish down the street. My husband and I sold our home and moved into an integrated neighborhood about six minutes out the front door [of Focus: HOPE's offices]. Now I didn't want to ask anybody to do anything I wasn't going to do myself. If I was going to talk about integration, I was going to live it.

My mother hired an attorney to take my five children away. My father-in-law disowned us and my brother-in-law, who was an engineer, asked me to use my maiden name so I wouldn't embarrass the family. It was not lack of love; they thought I had absolutely flipped out. My youngest was three; the oldest was 11. My mother made me a stronger person and she made me a leader and I give her lots of credit. She changed and became a very strong supporter. I think she was really testing to see if I knew what I was doing. My brother-in-law apologized last year. He said he's sorry for all of the pain he's caused me all those years.

It was difficult times. I mean you lose a lot of friends along the way.

Not everyone has to face such resistance from their

family and loved ones. Derek and Dawn Batts, a husband and wife team that together a financial services company, Union Heritage Capital Management, say working together is a real advantage.

We definitely understand the vision, which makes it a lot easier and more motivating day to day. I don't have to explain why I'm working late or he doesn't have to explain why he's working on a presentation, or why he's reading stock reports or financial news updates on the computer at 9:00 at night. We don't have to deal with that.

We also travel together. It becomes an issue when one person is traveling all the time doing presentations, or getting the business, and the other person is at home.

Most entrepreneurs can recount at least one story about a family member or friend who gave them an "armchair quarterback" coaching session from the sidelines on some aspect of their business. It almost seems as if being an entrepreneur gives others permission to submit their opinions – from the most well-intentioned observation to the most spiteful criticism.

The effects of the observations that can come from family and friends will vary. Since there is usually enough conflict within a business to fully engage most entrepreneurs, they look to their personal lives as a refuge from the madness. Business owners without a support system in place can crack under the constant spotlight of criticism. Others thrive on the "me against the world" scenario.

Entrepreneurs typically deal with input from others a gut level, merely reacting to statements and opinions, rarely if ever managing those reactions. Without managing their reactions, entrepreneurs can find that their confidence is undermined. Identifying the source, nature and proximity of negative energy and dealing with it is an essential step on the spiritual path of the entrepreneur.

In This Corner – The Advisor

Humans have a basic need for security that drives most of their decisions. They live in places that don't excite them; they eat things they don't like; and they work jobs they can't stand, all in the name of security. They cling to "the known," even as evidence mounts that the things they believe will provide them security don't come with guarantees.

After-September 11th, America's perception of safety became more on par with the rest of the world. Americans became aware that security is, at best, a tenuous intersection of chance and precaution. We get warnings every day about the effects of coffee or carbs or chocolate, only to learn the next day of their possible health benefits. The regular nine to five jobs that people complain about yet cling to are rapidly disappearing. Workers whose job was their "ball and chain" suddenly find themselves free, clueless and scared.

There are those who are the most comfortable in that limbo between committing to their current job and creating another situation for themselves. When they see other ordinary people committing themselves to their dreams, and fail to do likewise, their complaints and excuses become hollow. One of the most difficult things in the world is to move from the sidelines onto the field, yet there are entrepreneurs who do it every day. It is often easier to criticize those risk takers than to assume the risk. Genuine concern can motivate advice from family and friends, but sometimes criticism is also a natural way for those who criticize to deal with their own fears of starting something themselves. Other critics may be playing "on the field," but their vision and values may be incompatible with your success.

Sheila Washington heads the Washington Consulting Group, a lean East Coast strategic consultancy with a blue chip global client list. Others encouraged her to grow, but her philosophy is "bigger is not necessarily better."

So many women get sucked into believing the only model of success is having a big business. They are told, "You've got to take on office space and hire a lot of people." Often times they go through the painful process of having to downsize the office space and lay off people or fire them and it was because they lost sight of their vision. They let somebody else convince them that this is what success looks like. I've been very clear that only I can define success for me, and I'm pretty clear on what that looks like.

And In This Corner – The Entrepreneur

As the saying goes, it takes two to tango. Entrepreneurs have several characteristics that can make them more defensive of any criticism – even constructive criticism. Input and opinions from others do not have to automatically cause a conflict. Entrepreneurs can choose to take the words of their family and friends with a grain of salt – or ignore them altogether.

People As An Extension of God

Managing our relationships with equal measures of compassion and candor, forgiveness and functionality can help us to remove some of the tension that can wear us down.

From a spiritual perspective, other people are an opportunity for an extension of God in our lives. Beyond our limited interpretations of their actions, others can be remarkable teachers and guides in the game of life. Even those whose actions we view as negatively impacting us serve a powerful purpose. They show us how to allow negative energy to exist in our lives without giving it power. Forgiveness and acceptance are the key to living powerfully in a world that sometimes seems to arrange itself specifically to make us unhappy. Relationships are the bedrock of our existence.

Three-Circle Support Structure

The first step towards effectively managing relationships in support of your entrepreneurial path is to create a structure. Ideally, it should be a structure that is not dependent upon a particular type of relationship. It should be flexible and fulfill the specific purpose of facilitating the best support. One such model is the Three Circle Support Structure.

Imagine a circle, within which you would place the friends and family, mentors and protégées who have the largest stake in your life. Their praises and their criticisms can make a difference to you. You truly care what they think. Outside the circle is everyone else. That circle is called your Circle of Community.

Within the Circle of Community are two additional inner circles with a common area. One inner circle is your Circle of Business. People within your Circle of Business are directly associated with you in your role as an entrepreneur. They are employees, vendors, suppliers and colleagues.

The other inner circle is the Circle of Balance. The family and friends from whom you try to gain balance and spiritual fulfillment should be placed within the Circle of Balance. Often people in your Circle of Balance include your spouse, children, close friends and your spiritual family.

The area that intersects your Circle of Balance and your Circle of Business is called the Core. Those special individuals who fit in both categories should be placed in the Core.

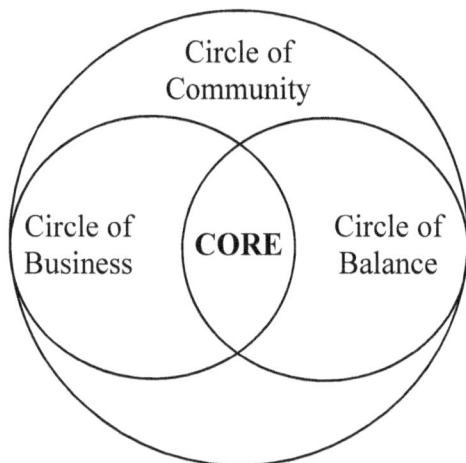

The Classification By Response Table

How will you know who fits in which circle? There is a separate exercise that can assist you in the process. By completing the Classification by Response Table, you can begin to understand where individuals fit in the structure by mapping the quality and type of your relationships. Instead of simply listing the people in your life, you can generate additional useful information by categorizing your perception of their position with regard to supporting your business goals. Each person in your life can be classified as having one of four responses to you as an entrepreneur:

- **Negative/Active** – they frequently offer negative and non-supportive comments
- **Negative/Passive** – while not very vocal or verbal, they often express a quiet disapproval of your choice to be in business
- **Positive/Active** – they are fully in support of you as an entrepreneur
- **Positive/Passive** – they either offer silent support of you being an entrepreneur or they are disinterested

Once you map out where and how you believe the people in your life exist within your personal support system, you can manage those relationships.

Negative Classification

For those people in the Negative/Active and Negative/ Passive categories, you can practice dynamic forgiveness. Write them letters in which you apologize to them for making them out to be the villains in your life. Let them know that you are interested in fulfilled relationships with them and that you can agree to disagree in the area of your business.

If they are within the Circle of Balance, articulate your expectations and promise to make the adjustments and compromises required to focus on allowing them to be the spiritual extension in your life. If they are within the Circle of Business, give them the space to make a real contribution to your business, instead of just comments. Listen to their words with new ears so that you can discover the value of their input. Commit yourself by allowing them to hold you to your promises. Just the act of writing the letters should begin to produce some results in your relationships and lighten the load in your life. For an extra bonus, mail the letters.

Positive Classification

For the people in the Positive/Active and Positive/ Passive categories, you can practice dynamic gratitude. Write them letters truly acknowledging the gift they have been in your life and letting them know how much their support means to you. If any of them are living vicariously through you, encourage them to take their own leaps of faith. Allow them to contribute fully to you by inviting them to help you stay on task with your goals. They are in your life trying to help you to achieve your greater good.

Mardi Woods, the Warm Spirit health and beauty product consultant, illustrates the importance of a support network.

I had a couple of good coaches when I was making my transition from corporate America to entrepreneurship. They were personal friends of mine who had already made their transition. [They] provided me with support, prayers, encouragement and the "how to" in making the leap of faith. They helped me take my dream and desire of wanting to do something that would enable me to have a home based business and spend more time with my kids to doing something about it. Their support, which included talks, walks, and prayers, was invaluable to me.

The people within the Core are vitally important to your spiritual well being. They are important companions on the path from fear to faith. They are your starting team, your All-Star lineup. Your objective is to have as many people from the Positive/Active quadrant in your Core as possible. If you find that you have few relationships that fit into your Core, you should take steps to create them. While the structure for creating those linkages will be discussed in more detail in Step Ten, you can begin the research now for building your Core relationships as a valuable resource for your spiritual path as an entrepreneur.

Toolkit

The opinions of others affect us in unexpected and negative ways unless they are managed. Fill in the names of people in your life in the Classification by Response Table below to help reduce some of your stress.

	Positive	Negative
Active	1. _____ 2. _____ 3. _____ 4. _____ 5. _____	1. _____ 2. _____ 3. _____ 4. _____ 5. _____
Passive	1. _____ 2. _____ 3. _____ 4. _____ 5. _____	1. _____ 2. _____ 3. _____ 4. _____ 5. _____

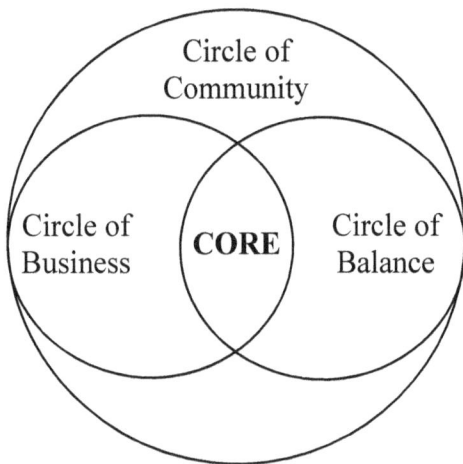

Circle of Community

Circle of Business

CORE

Circle of Balance

Journaling is prayer.

Manage Your Relationships

Contemplate your Three-
Circle Support Structure. Jot
down actions you need to
take based on your insights.

Homework

Meditation

The way you activate the seeds of your creation is by making choices about results you want to create. When you make a choice, you mobilize vast human energies and resources which otherwise go untapped. All too often people fail to focus their choices upon results and therefore their choices are ineffective. If you limit your choices only to what seems possible or reasonable, you disconnect yourself from what you truly want, and all that is left is a compromise.

Questions to consider

1 What situation led to your becoming an entrepreneur?

2 Was entrepreneurship a conscious choice, a matter of circumstance or a combination of the two?

3 Why are you still in business?

4 What criteria do you use to make the major decisions in your life?

5 What do you notice about the conversation you had with yourself when answering the questions above?

Step 5: Choose
Your Life

"The power to choose." We may have heard this phrase before. Yet there is a great deal to be learned in examining the meaning and implications of those words.

Every day, we are faced with a world full of options. What health care plan should you choose? What is the best mobile phone carrier and call plan? Which of the hundreds of available cable channels should you watch? Which of the 200 breakfast cereals on the grocery store shelf are the best for your children?

We are inundated with so much information that the process of selection has become a burden.

According to "The Tyranny of Choice", an April 2004 *Scientific American* article by Barry Schwartz, the overwhelming number of options, coupled with the pressure to make the "right choice" can lead to a decreased quality of life. "Although some choice is undoubtedly better than none, more is not always better than less," says Schwartz.

Another element that increases the stress we feel when making choices is the market culture that ties our choices into our identities. Everyday products – the car we drive, the mutual fund we buy, our choice in jeans, and even the food we eat – are a reflection of our status, our attractiveness, our intelligence, or our sense of family responsibility. With such high stakes on the line, the cost of making a bad choice looms large in our consciousness. Each choice must support our image of ourselves. Given the risk, our rationale for choosing can become more important than the choice itself. In fact for many of us, the choice is made by comparing reasons for one option against another. If we find ten reasons to support option A and twelve reasons for option B, we choose option B. We place the responsibility of our choices on our matrix of rationales rather than on ourselves.

Bearing total responsibility for our choices puts a strain on the process, a strain that we resist. However, there is immense power in making choices, if we own those choices.

Consider the choice to marry someone. There are several great reasons to choose marriage. You may have the same values. You may be physically attracted to one another. You may wish to have children and a lifelong companion. You may be interested in marriage to become more economically stable. Whatever the reason, marriage is the type of choice that has serious implications for your family, your health, your wealth and your happiness.

Let's say you meet someone and find that everything is aligned: you are physically, spiritually, emotionally, and financially compatible. You both want two children and a permanent traveling companion. You can play tennis together every Sunday afternoon and you both enjoy rainy nights with cold pizza and a good movie. You even get along his family and friends. Yee-ha, it's time to get hitched! Right?

During the wedding, you declare to God and to your community that you choose this person to spend the rest of your life with. For many, that scenario is simply a lie – not an intentional lie, but a fantasy nonetheless. For them, the promise to spend the rest of their life is dependent upon the reasons they choose their mate. They can stay married as long as their spouse stays attractive, physically whole, and interested in two children, traveling, and the occasional cold pizza and a movie. If any of those conditions changes, then the marriage is vulnerable. If the spouse cheats or the in-laws get out of control, then divorce becomes a viable option.

But there is a deeper level of choice. Sure, you can

find someone who shares your goals and values and is equally thrilled by the cold pizza and a movie scenario, but instead of making those factors the glue that keeps you in the marriage, you can choose to make the commitment to the marriage the focus – one that is independent of the reasons you initially chose that mate. Your spouse will not always be as attractive as they once were. You may not be able to have children and traveling may not always fit on the agenda. Basically, things happen. Situations change. The only constants in a marriage are those that we construct in the form of commitments. This is true of other life choices as well.

Choice Begins Creation

Choice is "responsible intention." It is our consciousness, our responsibility to our intentions, that brings power to our ability to choose. It is our consciousness that makes us human and gives us the power to choose and therefore to create. We must take responsibility, own our thoughts and choices. Responsible intention is just the starting point for all creation. Action must follow commitment. From there we can expect outcomes – or creation. Another way of thinking about this process is to follow the internal process of conscious, responsible intention that drives external action and leads to material results. In its simplest form, the process of creation is known as the Be-Do-Have paradigm.

The Be-Do-Have Paradigm

"Being" something involves conscious, responsible intention. It is the foundation of our choices. Ultimately, it is choice that defines our reality. Unfortunately, most people think that their reality is created by what they "have"—external things like more money, a shinier car, or more time. With these things, they can "do" everything that is important in their lives—finally write that novel, ask that cute girl out on a date, or start their business. They believe that doing these things will allow them to "be" what they really want to be—creative, loved, successful, or happy.

Actually, it works in the opposite direction. Being drives everything. Being a thing—whether its happy or sad, successful or self-destructive—naturally generates a series of actions. When you are happy, you do things that happy people do. You smile, you may let a car move in front of you in traffic with no resentment, you give compliments, you may even sing or skip. You probably don't even plan these actions in advance, they just flow from you as a result of your being happy. These types of actions produce tangible results in the world. Many times, the way people are—call it their attitude or mindset—creates positive reactions from others that make it easier for them to get the job, the date acceptance, or start the business. A negative mindset can generate the opposite result.

Choices are simple creative acts. As with all creations, there are two elements to a choice. The first element is your generation of the choice. The second element is the support of your choice in the world. I am not saying that being successful or happy or loving takes the world's permission, I am saying that the entire process of being-doing-having includes a tangible result in the world. There are many "enlightened" folks that just stop with being and never produce the things that they want. You are a spiritual being, but you are playing on a material plane. Part of the lesson of our being here is to learn to *intentionally* manifest your reality on this plane.

Internal Generation and External Support of the Choice

One of the most important things to remember about initiating a choice, or being, is that it does not necessitate a great deal of support from the outside world. It is creation. Think of a blank palette or empty notebook. The only boundary is the medium, and even that can be altered. You can choose to be successful when you are homeless. You can choose to be loving even if you have been abused.

I repeat, your creations do not need to be initially supported by the outside world. However, to the extent that they are not supported by the outside world, your choices require a higher level of being and doing from you.

To express this dynamic graphically, think of choice as a circle. If your parents are wealthy, you have a great job, and you are conventionally attractive, then you have a certain level of support in the external world that says you should be a successful person engaged in successful person activities and having successful person things. While this is all too often not the case—particularly the being part—for our example let's say that 75% your success (your being, doing and having it) is supported by the outside world and 25% of it is generated by you.

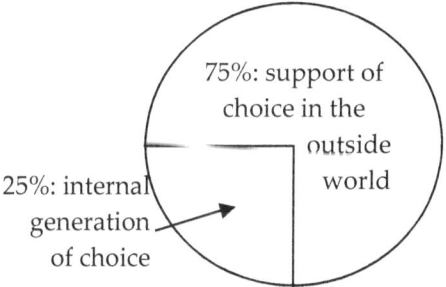

Conversely, if you are homeless, without a college education, with abusive parents and a racial minority, a different dynamic could be the case.

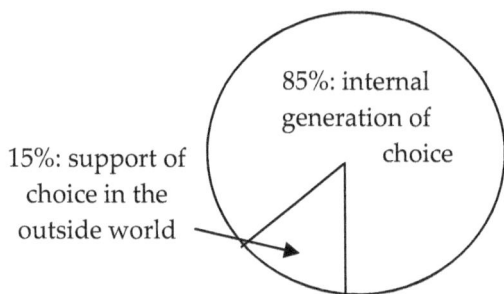

15%: support of
choice in the
outside world

85%: internal
generation of
choice

This dynamic does not mean that success is impossible. Chris Gardner was a homeless, African American, single father without a college degree. He bathed his son in public sinks and fed him in soup kitchens. From the moment he saw the wealth that being a stockbroker could provide, he became wealthy and conceptualized a pattern of actions (getting a job as a stockbroker) that could produce the material goods that he wanted. He did not actually get his job as a stockbroker until—against the odds—someone reacted to who Chris was being and hired him. Eventually, Chris worked his way up, started his own firm and became a multimillionaire whose life story was made into a film, *The Pursuit of Happyness*.

Being

Chris Gardner's remarkable story started with being. The first step that he took in being was *visualizing*. He formed a mental picture of himself as wealthy. You can supplement your mental picture with real pictures as tangible anchors. The second step he took was *believing* that picture. There was little support in the outside world for that belief, so he had to generate it within himself consistently over time. The third step he took was *submitting* to this way of being. To submit is to yield oneself to the power or authority of another. In this case, your everyday way of being yields to a new way of being.

I use the word submission rather than commitment because yielding in this way invites a spiritual element. If the way of being that you are willing to yield your life to is aligned with spiritual purpose, then its potential to exist is multiplied exponentially. You will have learned one of the most important lessons of creation.

Doing

When you are being something, you will naturally do the things that are consistent with that being. If you are a someone who is being self-destructive, you do not have to plot out actions that will support your self-destruction. If you examine your life, you will find that you are not eating right or exercising, that you are attracted to and attracting individuals that are not raising you to your highest level, and that your job is a miserable one. You may think that there is a conspiracy to sabotage your life and you are right. You are the author and architect of that sabotage. You may do things to help yourself, but if your doing is not grounding in who you are being, it has little effect.

Doing is not just about the actions you perform, it is also about what actions you allow yourself to receive. If you are among a group of gossipy people who always have something negative to say, that counts as part of your doing—even if you are not the one verbalizing the gossip. Inaction is action, and supports whatever you are being at the time.

Having

Having something is the end stage of the creative process. This stage takes the smallest amount of effort. Having is acceptance of a material thing— acknowledgement of its existence and understanding the process that it took to get there. Acknowledgement and understanding includes knowing the role of a higher power in producing that thing.

Having is also about freely sharing the material results. Some people have money, but no matter how much they have, they feel it is not enough—and certainly not enough to share. If you cannot share what you have (money, love, etc.), you do not believe you have the power to freely create it in your life. With that mindset, you block yourself from your ability to create.

Remember that your choices define your reality. This process is not happening as a result of reading this book, it has always been the case. You are where you are now because of your choices, conscious or unconscious. Your life will continue along a path created by your choices.

Entrepreneurship Is Living By Choice

As entrepreneurs, we have a structure for living with conscious, responsible intention. We create our incomes and the manner in which that income is generated. There is a contrast to the way we think and the way that some of our employees think. Many employees subconsciously transfer their permission to be happy, fulfilled, or effective in their job to their employer, their manager, or someone—anyone—else. They sometimes allow others to dictate whether they have the freedom to be excellent in their job. They allow others to determine what they are to do and how much they are paid to do it. Entrepreneurs choose their work and their pay.

The spiritual opportunity of the entrepreneurial choice is realized when we are completely conscious and intentional about the results we intend to create. The knowledge that our choices are grounded in a deeper spiritual process helps to eliminate fear in the decision-making process. We are "walking by faith, not by sight." Intention and consciousness clear your mind of the clutter and stress of everyday life that can lead to fear. The consequences of past concerns fade away as you open yourself to the unlimited possibility of the present. Conscious choice is the pivotal step we have the power to make—every day—on our path from fear to faith.

Toolkit

Our lives are the result of our choices. Use the formula below and "responsible intention" to construct your choices and to take your business (and your life) to the next level.

	BE		DO		HAVE	
	I make the choice to be...	by taking total responsibility for...	I am committed to ...	by ...	I will achieve ...	by...
Choice 1						
Choice 2						
Choice 3						

Choose Your Life

Look at your business and examine those areas where you have allowed circumstances to choose your results. Identify at least three areas and write down the impact – both positive and negative – of the results you have gotten. Be prepared to share your results with those in your Core.

Homework

When the drumbeat changes, the Dance changes.

African proverb

Reason is an action of the mind; **knowledge** is a possession of the mind; **but**

Faith

is an **attitude** of the person.

It means you are prepared to stake yourself on something being so.

Michael Ramsey

Meditation

We are not valuable because we are a member of a certain group or because we call God by a certain name. We are not valuable because we follow a guru or observe a certain diet. We are valuable because we are a spark of the divine. And the only thing Gurus, priests, rabbis and elders can do for us is point us back in the direction of home, and home is, of course, within.

Darren John Main

Questions to consider

1 Does God exist, who or what is God and what is God's relationship to you?

2 Does God have any rules, and if so, what are they?

3 Why are you here on Earth?

4 What happens when you die?

5 What do you notice about the conversation you had with yourself when answering the questions above?

Step 6: Get Religion

There are thousands of different faith groups in the world today. Religion is an expression of our desire to connect to the Divine. This connection is as ethnically diverse and ingrained in various peoples as our language, the method by which we connect to each other. Religion is a cultural phenomenon, shaped by our ancestors, our environment and our need for comfort and control in a world that sometimes seems overwhelming. Religion is a man-made construct, subject to the imagination, inspiration and limitations of men. It is a structure for processing spirituality.

Dr. Guérin Montilus, professor of cultural anthropology at Wayne State University, has a useful definition of spirituality that distinguishes it from the religious context usually surrounding it. Spirituality is defined as "the integrating power, the merging faculty, which pulls together all parts of our cosmos. It is the enlightenment which dissolves the boundaries of our multiplicity, and fades away all internal dissension. Then there is no distinction, no separation, but only oneness." Spirituality is not theological, it is ontological. It is the very nature of our being beyond our physical selves.

Spirituality is a totally different domain than religion. It is not dependent upon culture, needs or comfort because it is not of humans. Spirituality is the Creator's extension toward us; religion is our extension towards the Creator. But we need both. In fact, spirituality is interpreted through our limited lens and integrated into ourselves and our lives as religion.

For some who have been turned off by organized religion, that statement may be hard to hear. Consultant Sheila Washington shares a lot of people's frustration with religion.

I go to church and I walk in the door feeling good and I walk out feeling frustrated and just not in a good place because of the politics and all of the hoopla that seems to get in the way of the message.

All that is really necessary is for your religious structure to exist, to be bigger than you, and to involve other people. Without other people's involvement, there is no growth beyond your own knowledge and interpretation.

For those who regard their particular brand of religion as the only true path, that statement might be easy to misinterpret. In some ways, religion is the language we speak to God. There are certain nuances, denotations and connotations that are specific to each language, but the essence of communication is the same. Apple, *la pomme* and *tofaa* describe the same concept. But an apple is not any more inherently an apple than *une pomme*, or for that matter, *tofaa*. Rather than being attached to some inherent apple-ness, or for that matter, an inherent *tofaa*-ness, it serves us more to master our own language and respect the beauty of others than to limit a concept to the syllables that describe it.

Religion is a structure for processing spirituality. The root word of religion is the Latin word *religare*, meaning to tie back or to bind. Religion, through rituals and regularly practiced observances, binds spirituality to our daily lives.

Religion is an individualized expression. Within any church, synagogue, mosque or shrine, there are individual adherents making their own connection to the Source. If you are a Muslim, your experience of Islam is specific to you. No one else in the world has said exactly the prayers you have said or had exactly the experiences you have had, at the same time you have had them. The feelings of faith and submission are filtered through the individual lens of your own unique experience; as the eldest son, or the first grand-daughter, a native of Sierra Leone, or a native of Detroit.

Religion is a requirement for the spiritual path of the entrepreneur. Everyone interested in religion creates their own religious path, however most people affiliate themselves with an organized system of religion.

The higher purpose of organized religion is to create fellowship – to allow the faithful to share their religious experience, tradition and teachings with others. Some religions have thousands of years of tradition and history. Other newer religions offer a fresh perspective on our purpose, on this earth and beyond.

Consider exploring the diversity and individuality of religion in order to gain an understanding of its innate humanness. There are many people who have been swayed on their spiritual path because they have stumbled on the limitations of religion, but embracing those limitations can allow us to be free to worship in our own way—and to respect the rights of others to do the same.

As a cultural expression, religion gives us rules to live by – usually rules set in the context of the society in which it was developed, using the language of that society to communicate to the Creator. Like language, the religion to which we subscribe gives us a context for living. Just as the Eskimo have nearly 30 different words for "snow," religions tend to focus on specific aspects of a particular society's needs. Like language, religion can become so much a part of our expression of truth that we forget it is just an expression of truth, not ultimate Truth. We forget that although others may not speak our religious language, they still are communicating with the Creator. If we shift our focus away from the language and toward the communication, we can find aspects of spirituality.

Common Elements of Religious Systems

Although there are many different traditions, there are certain common elements across most of the world's religious systems. In *Ritual and Religion in the Making of Humanity*, anthropologist Roy Rappaport identified religion's most universal elements: "the sacred," "the numinous," "the occult" and "the divine." These elements, when fused in ritual, produce "the holy."

The sacred is the part of religion that is expressed in language. It is the oaths, the liturgy, the prayers, the texts, and the commandments. It is the logic and rules of a religion, and the sacred gives us a medium to pass on our religious heritage.

The **numinous** is the feeling we get in our religious experience. It exists beyond our normal conversation. It is the peace we may feel after we leave the Catholic confessional, or the anticipation we may experience at the beginning of a Vodun initiation. The numinous takes religion out of heads and puts it in our hearts. It breathes life into the texts and makes religion personal, relevant and real.

The **occult** is the capacity for religion to have power and effect in the world and in our lives. From baptismal ceremonies and communion to smoke baths and fasts, occult activities are intended to usually transform, purify or strengthen those who participate in them. Most religions also have some sort of occult artifacts, such as crucifixes, ju-jus, charms or amulets. The occult is the physical sign of spiritual power. Its effectiveness is largely a function of our belief.

The **divine** are the spiritual beings to whom the religion refers. They are gods and goddesses, ancestral spirits and the Holy Spirit. The divine can be as impersonal as Nature or the Force. The divine can also have all the personal characteristics of the God of the Old Testament, Shango or Zeus. The divine is our ultimate Source, and how we conceive of that Source plays a major role in who we choose ourselves to be.

The **holy** is the total religious phenomenon. It is

the sacred, the numinous, the occult and the divine woven together through ritual and belief. As a means to process the spiritual, the holy is both a communal creation and a personal creation. Religion is one of the most meaningful products of our culture and personal experiences.

Creation and Entrepreneurship

While religion is a significant product of our creative energies, entrepreneurship is other significant product we create. As with religion, entrepreneurship is co-creation with our Source. There is an exchange in the dynamics of spiritual entrepreneurship – between Creator and entrepreneur, entrepreneur and customer, supplier and entrepreneur, and community and entrepreneur. As U.S. Anderson writes in his book, *Three Magic Words*, the basis of business is the Law of Mutual Exchange.

> *The Law of Mutual Exchange is the law of morality, of sin and punishment, of righteousness and reward. How best can we serve? The answer is by creating, never by competing. We serve neither ourselves nor humanity by competing for another man's job, another manufacturer's market, another man's business. We serve by creating new jobs, new markets, new means, and new methods. The magic that makes each of us what he is springs from an inexhaustible source. We are creative*

creatures, umbilically tied to the creative power of God.
We create by our thoughts, miraculously, each moment
of every day.

Religion – any religion – can provide an important context for business. It provides guidelines for the tough decisions and challenging situations that are the entrepreneurial experience. Most of the messy issues that take our time and our energy are people issues — things that go beyond the balance sheets and income statements. Dealing with the personal issues that spill out into the workplace and the everyday humanness of our daily interactions without losing focus requires spiritual infrastructure. Without it, we can center ourselves on our business and lose perspective.

It is natural to need something in our lives that is bigger than ourselves. Without a spiritually-focused religious base, you can fall into the trap of making your business your religion. It is perfectly okay to experience your business as a calling and to feel a sense of connectedness to the higher purpose of your work, but when you see your business as the end and not the means, you can find yourself devoted to something that ultimately cannot fulfill you. You may also lose the ability to know when it is time to move to the next opportunity because you are too attached to the way things are.

Religion ultimately allows you to wear the world as a loose garment. It is your compass, your true North and what lights your path as you move from fear to faith.

Toolkit

Religion is a requirement for the spiritual path of the entrepreneur. Write down your current structure for processing spirituality in your life.

Journaling is prayer.

Compare and Contrast

Research a religious system whose views you do not share. List ten elements that your share with that system and ten things that are different from what you believe. Jot down any insights you gained from this exercise.

Homework

Meditation

Don't think you can attain total awareness and whole enlightenment without proper discipline and practice. This is egomania.

Appropriate rituals channel your emotions and life energy toward the light.
Without the discipline to practice them, you will tumble constantly backward into darkness.

Lao-Tzu

Questions to consider

1 What are your religious rules and rituals?

2 What are your business rules and rituals?

3 Do they intersect? If so, how?

4 What are your "good" habits – those that help you to move your life forward?

5 What do you notice about the conversation you had with yourself when answering the questions above?

Step 7: Connect to Your Source

There are people who capitalize on the opportunity of religion, but many do not. As an individual expression, religion provides the opportunity to link with the Source in a way that is dynamic, meaningful and satisfying.

For some, religion is an automatic routine. It is comfortable in its familiarity and fits neatly into their lives. They go to the same church, sit in the same pew and speak the same prayers their parents and grandparents spoke. They pray the same prayer every night before every meal and before they go to bed. Religion is compartmentalized into Sunday service and mumbled words at the appropriate time.

For others, religion is something they are always going to "get around to." They are dissatisfied with the beliefs they grew up with, yet they have not taken the time to discover their own path. They reflect on their religion during a holiday or at a funeral, but it is as random as their passing thoughts.

Religion is a resource for entrepreneurs, a resource that many only partially utilize. It can provide objective guidelines to keep our businesses (and our lives) on track. It can "fill the well," sustaining our connection to the Divine, even as many of life's pressures drain us. It can allow us to handle risk and challenges. It can be the staff that holds us up, and the rudder that helps us to find our way. Religion is an essential part of creating the staying power needed by entrepreneurs.

How do we create a dynamic, meaningful and satisfying connection with our Creator? What structure would facilitate a vibrant expression of our faith? Begin by creating and implementing habits that help to produce a practical relationship with God. Habits shape the quality of our lives, and adherence to our habits produces consistent results. A child who develops the habit of flossing daily and brushing their teeth after every meal is more likely to maintain a healthy smile throughout their lifetime. A college student who creates the habit of studying the correct material two hours every day will probably find academic success. A lifetime tobacco smoker who goes through two packs a day will probably encounter health issues. Habits, whether progressive or regressive, are the outlines of our future.

There are habits that can help you to create a practical connection to Spirit and to develop your own religious system. They are grouped into communion habits and fellowship habits. Communion habits help you build your direct connection to God. Fellowship habits help you to create a community to share religious experiences, traditions and teachings. Both are necessary for a balanced religious life. Communion is the primary category because it involves activities that develop an unfiltered and deeply personal spiritual connection with the Source. Activities in the fellowship category are also important because they help access insights beyond our individual experiences.

The Communion Habits

There are six communion habits that are of particular benefit to those on the spiritual path of the entrepreneur. They are as follows:

1. Ask the questions (prayer)
2. Get the answers (meditation)
3. Experience God daily
4. Visualize the outcome
5. Exercise your intuition
6. Do something different

Ask the Questions

It is often said that prayer is the medium for miracles. This is because prayer is acknowledgement of the power of God. Prayer is an act of submission and supplication to a Higher Power. Where else could you turn to ask the questions you need to ask? Most of us are in the habit of blocking our blessings with fear and doubt. When you develop the habit of prayer and witness its results, your faith will be strengthened. With increased faith, you will notice that your days become easier and your challenges less daunting. The habit of prayer is the habit of building trust in God's Divine Order.

Get the Answers

Meditation is the medium for insight. It is the intentional shifting of consciousness that occurs when we deeply relax and allow ourselves to simply be. With practice, meditation allows us to see beyond the veil of our ego and connect with the Universal Mind. Many of us on the spiritual path understand ourselves as part of a unified whole. We are comfortable with the concept that our bodies are not our boundaries. The gift of meditation is in experiencing a profound connectedness with everything – beyond the theoretical – and understanding that connectedness as Truth. Experiencing ourselves as one gives us access to Infinite

Intelligence. The habit of meditation is the habit of experiencing the Divine in you.

Experience God Daily

There is an interesting quote in Alice Walker's *The Color Purple*. "I think it pisses God off if you walk by the color purple in a field somewhere and don't notice it."

If you take the time to really observe your environment, you would be astonished at the beauty and majesty that surrounds you. Observe the miracle of a baby's fingernails or an octogenarian's eyes. Notice a small dandelion that is able to burst through a tiny crack in the concrete. These small spaces in life are places where you can experience a tangible sense of God's presence. When you feel disconnected to God, concentrate on opening yourself up to these experiences. Creating the habit of experiencing God daily creates the habit of experiencing the Divine in the world – and even in your business.

"You're relying on your faith to jump into something you have a lot less security about than when you were working for someone," says Domineca Neal. "But the part that was most impactful is when you actually see your dreams come to fruition. On one hand, you have your faith and you know that it's key to bringing your dreams to fruition, but you're still amazed when it becomes reality."

Visualize the Outcome

Visualization is the medium for manifestation. Performance-oriented achievers commonly use visualization to align their minds and their bodies toward a specific goal. It is a tool that can be used by swimmers and sculptors, chefs and cellists, actors and activists. Visualization involves seeing – with the mind's eye – a desired outcome. The key to effective visualization is repetition and detail. Professional basketball players visualizing their next game see their performance in the specific sports arena they'll play their next game in. They imagine themselves wearing the uniform that they will wear that night. They conjure up all the sights, sounds and smells of game time. Because we are a part of the Universal Mind, we manifest those things that we focus upon. Usually our thoughts are too conflicted or distracted to be physically creative, but with focused intention and sincere belief, we can produce anything. Sometimes the things we produce are positive. Sometimes they are negative. The habit of visualization harnesses your ability to create whatever it is that you focus your mind upon.

It is important to note that visualization does not work without a sincere belief in the outcome. Self-doubt—even subconscious self-doubt—erodes and negates the power of your focused intention. Simple visualization exercises can help you to build your faith in your power to bring your vision into being and therefore increase your capacity to manifest your thoughts in physical form.

Visualization Exercise: Close your eyes and clear your mind. Imagine a small red ball in your hands. Feel its weight and its texture. Is it soft, or hard? Is it shiny or dull? Dirty or clean? Is it smooth or is there a pattern you can see and feel? Is it heavy or light? Is there any writing on the ball? Does the ball give when squeezed or does it stay firm? How else would you describe it?

Open your eyes, and remember the size, texture and color of the ball you visualized. Over the next few weeks, expect to encounter that ball in a real, physical form. You may pass by it as you drive down the street. Your child may bring it home. You may even be given the ball as a gift. Look for the ball – really expect it. Meditation, prayer, and additional visualization of that ball will help you slow down to notice its presence.

Exercise Your Intuition

Intuition and creativity are the language of Spirit. The left side of the brain is associated with logic and analysis. The right side of the brain is associated with creativity and intuition. In the western educational system, most of the subjects taught develop left-brain thinking, leaving our right brain overwhelmed by the dominance of our analytical minds. Music and art are excellent stimuli for the right hemisphere. These creative activities can help us to deepen our connection with our spiritual Source. Developing our intuition and natural psychic ability also gives the right brain a workout that can lead to a fuller experience of Spirit in our everyday lives. Exercising your intuition assists us in learning the language of the soul.

Intuition Exercise: Card reading is actually an intuition exercise. Thoroughly shuffle a deck of cards and place them face down in front of you. Pick up the first card. Try to visualize the suit of the card. Are you right? One by one, place the cards you guess incorrectly on the left side of the deck. Place the cards you guess correctly on the right side of the deck. How many cards did you get right? Which suits were easier to perceive? For an extra challenge, try to guess the exact card you are holding. Develop your skill by listening for that small, still voice inside. That voice gives you access to the vision you need as you make the tough decisions.

According to entrepreneur Dawn Batts, the goal is "being in tune so that you can hear. Sometimes in your business, you don't hear anything other than what you are focused on. So when I release that and let go, I'm more in tune to hear spiritual direction."

Do Something Different

Life gets lost in the routine of living. When we move from day to day in mind-numbing sameness, life can pass us as swiftly and silently as a river current. We wake up wondering where the last fifteen years went, unable to remember time's passage. The key to living fully, present in the moment, is to punctuate your moments with something exciting and different. If you've never tried a flaming shish kabob, dare to try it. If you've never seen the houses on the other side of town, go see them.

Once you develop the habit of breaking your routine, you have access to living fully in the present. The past and the future are only an illusion. The only time that actually exists is now. The only moment where you have the power to act is now. The realm in which God exists is the "infinite Now." If you are not living in the now, you can become stuck replaying what happened last week or you can become stressed out about the challenge that faces you next Wednesday. The habit of doing different things focuses our mind on the present and facilitates the habit of living in the now.

The Fellowship Habits

As entrepreneurs, we can easily stay in our loner rut. It seems easier to rely on ourselves for our needs and to close ourselves to the contributions of others. It can be a stretch to expose something as personal as our beliefs to someone outside our immediate circle of family and friends.

Try these three fellowship habits to facilitate community support of your religious path and your spiritual growth. They are:

1. Build your spiritual home
2. Tithe
3. Indulge your inner artist with an audience

Build Your Spiritual Home

Matthew 18:20 reads, "For where two or three are assembled in my name, I am there among them." There is power and affirmation in the gathering of like souls for a spiritual purpose. The habit of building your spiritual home, or the place where you worship with others, gives you access to your humanity. The first step is finding one that fits you. It is important that the spiritual home you choose is your choice – not the place you go because you've always gone there. Your spiritual home must educate you, challenge you, accept you as you are, and resonate with your belief system.

There are many different areas to explore and questions to ask in choosing your spiritual home. The list below is simply a place to begin.

- What is the religious doctrine?
- How is music used in the religious ritual?
- What educational support is offered?
- What is the preaching style of the spiritual leader(s)?
- Does the leadership reflect the makeup of the community in ethnic, gender and/or sexual orientation?
- What specific dogma and doctrine does the organization advocate?
- What level and type of outreach in the community does the organization practice?
- Is there any particular issue around which community activism is focused?
- Is support offered during important events such as weddings and funerals?
- Are there affiliated groups specifically dealing

with business ownership and/or wealth creation? Is there an existing group of entrepreneurs
on the spiritual path? Can you create one?

- What religious curriculum and activities does
  the organization offer for children?
- What is the size and history of the organization?

Once you have found your spiritual home, you'll
get the best results when you commit yourself to active participation in its growth. Participating in a spiritual home involves developing and demonstrating the
capacity for active service for the greater good. There
is an African word, *ubuntu*, which has roots in the
Zulu and Xhosa languages. It means humanity in the
context of others. The concept of *ubuntu* is translated
most elegantly in the phrase, "I am, because we are,
and because we are, I am." The habit of participating
in building your spiritual home is practicing *ubuntu*.

Tithe

Tithing is an act of love that releases us from our at-
tachment to scarcity and opens us up to receive. It is
the medium of abundance. It is not something done
under duress. Coerced tithing is extortion and tithing
that does not allow us to meet our basic needs is an
unwise sacrifice. Tithes are given freely, and giving
them allows us to more clearly acknowledge the

Source of all prosperity. To truly understand the dynamic of tithing, it is necessary to understand the nature of money.

Money is commonly defined as a medium that can be exchanged for goods and services, used as a measure of value on the market. Gold, an officially issued coins or notes, or checking accounts or other readily liquefiable forms – these are all used as money. But the dollar bill or gold coin you thought was money isn't really money at all. It is a form of exchange. Money is a medium, an intervening substance through which something else is transmitted or carried on. Therefore, money is a vehicle – a vehicle for energy to flow. Dr. Caroline Myss (myss.com), the world-renowned author and healer, defines money as follows:

> *Money is a neutral substance that flows into and out of our lives, taking its direction from our intentions regarding it. It is those intentions that alter the neutral energy of money. Tribal beliefs and ideas greatly influence our relationship to money.*

> *We often allow money to substitute for life energy, frequently with negative consequences. A result being, every dollar we spend becomes an unconscious expenditure of energy. Scarcity of money can translates into a scarcity of energy in the body.*

Your challenge is to achieve a relationship with money separate from your life force. The more impersonal your relationship with money is, the more likely you are to direct its energy appropriately in your life.

An organic and healthy relationship to money is natural abundance. Here are the steps to bring this energy to your life:

- View money as simply another kind of energy that flows into and out of your life.

- Maintain a relationship with money that is without guilt.

- Operate from the viewpoint that the more you create the more there is for everyone.

- Get past the outdated notion that one must be poor to be spirituul.

These perceptions must be at the core of your energy system before natural abundance will be manifested on a physical/material level.

"The one thing I can remember my parents saying is that God will not be able to give you any blessings if your hands are closed," says consultant Sheila Washington. "So you need to be generous in all that you do and as your hands are open, your blessings will come. That has really been my life experience."

Tithing has a communal component. It is money being invested for the benefit of everyone, not just yourself. The act of tithing demonstrates the process of creation – the Be-Do-Have paradigm discussed in Step Five. It is a twist on the *ubuntu* concept. I have, because we have, and because we have, I have. The habit of tithing generates abundance.

Indulge Your Inner Artist with an Audience

Inside each of us is a creative spirit that is manifested in any number of ways. We are singers, writers, dancers and visual artists, waiting to be discovered or longing for more attention. A fellowship centered on creativity helps you to connect with your own soul and the souls of others. It is easy to create this fellowship. It can be done in the preparation of a meal, in a karaoke outing, or while coloring with your child. A surprise birthday party can be a dramatic production that allows you to create.

Certainly, there are many opportunities to share your creativity at your business. Allowing your creative juices to flow while working with others gives you access to a deep level of intimacy with a crowd of thousands or with just one other person. The habit of indulging your inner audience with an audience creates conversations of the soul.

Toolkit

Your walk on the spiritual path is a daily enterprise. The quality of your journey is a direct result of the structure you have created to keep a strong, viable connection to the Divine. Use the table below to evaluate which habits you already have and which you need to develop (NOTE: 1 = very consistently, 2 = consistently, 3 = inconsistently, 4 = very inconsistently, and 5 = never).

Communion Habits	How consistently do you practice this habit?					Actions To Take	By When
Ask the questions (prayer)	1	2	3	4	5		
Get the answers (meditation)	1	2	3	4	5		
Experience God daily	1	2	3	4	5		
Visualize the outcome	1	2	3	4	5		
Exercise your intuition	1	2	3	4	5		
Do something different	1	2	3	4	5		
Build your spiritual home	1	2	3	4	5		
Tithe	1	2	3	4	5		
Indulge your inner artist with an audience	1	2	3	4	5		

Journaling is prayer.

Feel Your Power

Visualize a simple object as directed on page 116. Jot down your sightings of that object and be prepared to share them with your Core. **Homework**

Meditation

Integrity is often thought of as moral uprightness and steadfastness—making the "good" choices, doing the "right thing." In fact, it is far more than that. It is a home, an anchor, a created and continuing commitment—a way of being and acting that shapes who you are.

-- Landmark Education

Questions to consider

1. What areas of your life are "working"? What areas of your life are not "working"?

2. How often do you do what you say you will do, when you say that you will do it, in those areas of your life that are working?

3. How often do you do what you say you will do, when you say that you will do it, in those areas of your life that are not working?

4. Are there any conversations you need to have or admissions you need to make with anyone in those areas of your life that are not working?

5. What do you notice about the conversation you had with yourself when answering the questions above?

Step 8: Pursue Integrity

Integrity is probably the single most confrontational concept for most people to explore. Not the comfortable, moralistic connotation of integrity, but the basic question; do you actually do what you say you are going to do – all the time.

Defining Integrity

Integrity as a moral construct is not nearly as daunting because it is so objective. We use a sliding scale – grade "on the curve." One lie is seen as more contemptible than another lie. The sliding scale is also time-dependent. A choice that was legitimate in the 1600's may be reprehensible today. Moral integrity is a function of context. In some religious systems, alcohol is seen as sinful; yet in others, alcohol is an integral part of the most sacred rituals. Integrity as a moral concept is better at separating the "good" from the "bad" than in providing a standard for living. Guilt is much more often a byproduct of misplaced moralistic integrity – rarely helpful in producing a life that works.

The concept of "integrity" as defined by the Landmark Education for personal development is a much more powerful. It is a concept that makes the student confront the notion of integrity and take personal responsibility. As humans, we are constantly doing things (and not doing things) that compromise our integrity. Think of integrity as the structure for making our lives work. If you do not exercise or eat right, the integrity of your structure for being healthy is unsound. It does not have to mean that you are bad, or weak, or suffering from moral corruption. It means that there is something clear and identifiable to be done – and you have the opportunity to make the choice to do it. Being out of integrity also weakens your structural foundation. If you do something against your neighbor, your understanding of spiritual law tells you that you are in fact, hurting yourself. There is a cost to be paid in your own quality of life for harming the growth, health or well being of another soul on the planet. You can numb yourself to the pain that comes from misalignment with those you harm, or you can take those steps that move you closer to wholeness by acting with integrity.

Often we can use lapses in our moralistic integrity

as an opportunity to wallow in self-pity, rather than an opportunity to take action. If you have ever found yourself spending energy beating yourself up about a mistake you made, you are doing just that. As entrepreneurs, we are probably our own worst critics. Self-bashing can become a habit; one that we don't give much thought but one which we can give lots of energy.

The spiritual path can be a way to free us from the self-bashing cycle. The constant search for perfection in one's actions is a clear indicator that a connection needs to be made with the Source. When we experience divine perfection, we can let go of the idea that we, ourselves, need to be perfect. We can, however, be committed to doing what we said we would do, when we said we would do it. We can notice when our actions are not aligned with who we've declared ourselves to be and make the appropriate adjustment. To be sure, the pursuit of integrity is a never-ending one. The more you open yourself up to the possibility that you are not perfect, the more imperfection you will find. Cleaning up that area of inauthenticity gives you access to a life that is not as weighted down with unacknowledged guilt. It has the effect of a spiritual cleansing.

Howard Bell, a serial entrepreneur and technology

park executive director, relates the struggle with integrity that led him to see that integrating religion with entrepreneurship means integrity.

When I first got into entrepreneurship, I struggled with the most interesting thing, which was selling the entrepreneurial product versus total honesty.

You've got to go in there with this concept of this website and sell them on the fact that we could do it – and frankly we didn't know we could do it. We thought that we could do it based on assumptions that we hadn't completely fleshed out.

From a faith-based perspective, I struggled with making a presentation about something that I didn't know 100% that I could do. I felt that I was sitting at the table and being dishonest and it ate at me. My voice was shaking. I had to call on God to understand that this was OK, that this was a regular part of the entrepreneurial process and that I had to somehow get by that.

Corporate Integrity

Corporate integrity must be approached from a different perspective than personal integrity. Corporations are legal entities that are created by man. They are not born with souls, nor are they born connected to the Universal Source. They have the ability to affect change in the world, but the accountability for their actions is not as securely tied to a single person as are the actions of an individual.

However, since they exist in the world, corporations are subject to Universal Law. Without sound integrity in its processes, its cash flow, its products and/or services, its people, and its public perception, divine order foretells that the corporation will fail. It is critical that you, as an entrepreneur, maintain the systemic integrity of your company. Do not make promises you can't keep, and when you do, apologize and make amends to those you have affected. Calculate the taxes you owe, pay them and be glad that you can. If you cannot pay, speak with the appropriate agency and make arrangements to pay on a schedule you can keep.

In running a corporation, you have a unique opportunity to achieve another level of integrity. You have the opportunity to allow your company to become a vehicle for the spiritual energy that increases the quality of life, raises the consciousness, or even transforms the mindset of the world. The business of a company is making money, but money is made from filling a basic need. Beyond the basics, there are higher needs to be fulfilled – the need to protect the environment, the need to connect, the need to create. Corporations can fill these needs.

Every corporation should have a vision that guides their mission – a higher possibility that can inspire anyone who reads it. It is important to note that integrity is an objective adherence to subjective values. Corporations should also have value statements that articulate their commitments and a plan for keeping them. One such example is Bolthouse Farms, a family-owned vegetable and produce enterprise. A *Business Reform* article described the company and its stand for integrity in business dealings.

> *In 1990, many of Bolthouse's competitors were moving in to Mexico in order to take advantage of the cheap labor and warm weather. Bolthouse Farms, seeing that staying out of the race south could have dire consequences for its bottom line, took steps to buy land and hired a consultant to advise on such a move.*

> *Assured from the start that the company would not be required to pay the usual bribes to the Mexican officials at the border, Bill sent some members of his management team to Mexico to assess the situation for themselves. When they returned, they reported that the assurance that they had received about the bribes had been faulty. Their competitors were already well established in the country and had been forced to pay out bribes in order to secure such a position. After hearing this news, an employee approached Bill and made a convincing*

case for how such bribes would be in direct conflict with the mission statement drafted just a few years before. In his wisdom and humility, Bill cancelled the planned move.

It took less than two years for Bill to see that God's providential hand had been involved in the deal the whole time. Right around 1992, every one of the farm's competitors was forced out of Mexico, and many lost a large amount of money in the process. Bolthouse Farms, however, was by this time already involved in the packaging and distribution of the baby carrots (having, ironically enough, poured the money that had been set aside for the move to Mexico into production of the baby carrots) and were well ahead of the competition by the time they retreated back into the states. The success of the baby carrots, then, was directly related to Bill and Co.'s attention to biblical principles and their collective desire to please the Lord even when it didn't initially seem convenient. (Copyright 2004, Business Reform Magazine)

Business Karma

The word "karma" comes from the Sanskrit verb kri, "to do." Karma is both action and reaction. Its essence is captured in the maxim, "As ye sow, so shall ye reap." It is the law of cause and effect. Because corporations operate "in the world," they are subject to universal law. As such, they can become vehicles for both positive and negative karma.

Karma's impact can be conceptualized as a ripple effect. Actions don't exist in a vacuum. They are imprinted on our minds (either consciously or subconsciously) and they affect our environment. For companies, the ripple effect becomes a lot more complex because the actions and reactions happen on many levels and involve many people. An automotive company may pollute the environment with the toxins that its products generate, but it also might employ thousands of people and help them to feed, clothe and shelter their families. A pharmaceutical company might spend hundreds of millions to discover a cure for particular disease, but its senior officers might not disclose the negative effects of a particularly profitable drug.

Corporations have the potential to affect millions. They operate without the benefit of a conscience, a soul or an intrinsic connection to the Universal Whole. Corporations are not inherently evil, nor are they inherently good. They are powerful vehicles for whatever possibilities their leadership wants to pursue. The challenge of being an entrepreneur is to not allow the business to overtake your humanity. If the game you are playing as a business owner is simply to generate the most profits, eventually you may do something that runs counter to what works for the planet. If you use your business to harm the planet, you will generate negative karma that will come back to the business and affect you or future leaders of your business.

Karma, Integrity and Atonement

In order for a business or organization to achieve its highest potential, it must achieve the state of integrity necessary to support that potential. Systemic integrity and the generation of positive karma are two important components to achieving that state. Another crucial component is atonement.

Great care must be taken to ensure that past misdeeds are acknowledged and corrected. There are corporations that have profited by taking the wealth of Holocaust victims. Eventually, without atonement, they must pay a price for their actions. Although millions have experienced unprecedented freedom on its soil, America itself is a country built on stolen land, by the stolen labor of stolen people. The magnitude of the karma debt of genocide and greed is greater than the country is able to even acknowledge, let alone repay.

Atonement is the only way to counteract the negative effects. Atonement is a rebalancing of karma, brought about by the power of love. The verb "atone" comes from the phrase "at one," meaning to reconcile, or make as one. The wholeness that this term infers is a state of love and balance so perfect that once it is achieved the original offense disappears. Atonement is the process by which such reconciliation is achieved. Atonement can therefore be an act of pure love made by an individual or entity that demonstrates, beyond the theoretical, the inherent oneness of all things. It is a denying of the individual ego and an affirmation of the universal spirit. For entrepreneurs, it is looking unflinchingly at the negative effects of the way you have done business and placing your highest priority on counteracting those effects. This is not done as an unselfish act, but as a selfless act, recognizing that the limited concept of "self" that our society has adopted is fundamentally untrue. We are, in truth, as one.

Toolkit

Your business can only be as successful as its infrastructure for integrity allows it to be. Use the structure below as a template to gauge the systemic integrity of the key areas of your business.

Area	Is It Operating in Integrity?	Required Tasks to Establish Integrity
People Management		
Cash Flow Management		
Operations Management		
Perceptions Management		
Product Management		

Toolkit (continued)

Your business can only be as successful as its infrastructure for integrity allows it to be. Use the structure below as a template to gauge the systemic integrity of the key areas of your business.

Area	Team	Budget	Deadline
People Management			
Cash Flow Management			
Operations Management			
Perceptions Management			
Product Management			

Clear the Air

Are there any conversations that you have been avoiding with anyone connected to your business. List them – all of them. Have the two easiest and the two toughest conversations before the next session. Be prepared to share your results and insights with your Core.

Homework

Meditation

It often seems easier not to move on; even the muck and mire in which we're stuck seems less fearful and less challenging than the unknown path ahead. Some people use faith as a reason to remain stuck. They often say, 'I have faith, so I'm waiting.' But faith is not complacent; faith is action. You don't have faith and wait. When you have faith, you move. Complacency actually shows lack of faith. When it's time to move in a new direction in order to progress, the right people will come to us.

Betty Eadie

Questions to consider

1. Which areas in your life are you convinced will never get better?

2. Do you remember a time when you still had hope about those areas? What happened?

3. What areas in your life are you committed to change?

4. Why do you believe you can change them?

5. What do you notice about the conversation you had with yourself when answering the questions above?

Step 9: Find Flow

There is no greater power than the power of faith in action, grounded with a spiritual connection, guided by integrity, and unaffected by fear. When you think of moments and movements in human history that helped to shape our collective consciousness, they are typically acts of faith, spiritually connected, fearless and operating in integrity. From the civil rights movement to Woodstock, it is the bold stand, the decisive stroke that creates new possibilities and opens our perspective on the world.

Faith as theory is comfortable. Untested faith relies on the power of Spirit and asks nothing of us. That's the faith that we feel on Sunday morning in church as the preacher reaches into our hearts and inspires us to be grateful for the wonderful lives we have.

Faith in action is less comfortable because it requires participation. It is not a spectator sport. It requires us to reach into our own hearts. When we are in a dark space we must call upon faith to find the light we need to guide ourselves.

As entrepreneurs, we are always in action. Sometimes we take actions that we are sure of. Sometimes we act in an attempt to get direction or clarity – leaping from a cliff and hoping we'll grow wings during our flight. Somewhere in the midst of it all, we are awakened to faith through our actions. It shows up sporadically – inevitably, given the fast pace of life. There's that quick hit of exhilaration when we find a way out of no way and make payroll. The phone call delivering the news awarding us the contract we did not think we would get. Faith occurs as evidence for our optimism. Faith is the spare tire when things break down.

There is so much that is really out of your control in running a business, says entrepreneur Howard Bell.

I can remember riding to work realizing that if this customer didn't pay today, that I'd have to give a speech to my staff that there would be no paychecks today. As you're riding to work and you realize that you've already begged the customer twenty times and they're going to do it whenever they get ready and they probably have another set of circumstances that is dictating whether they can pay you that has nothing to do with what you've done as much as whatever other things are out there that are controlling their ability to pay you. You realize that you might as well call on God because if God doesn't get that person the money, then you're not going to get it. At some point when you start feeling as an entrepreneur that you have less control than you just assumed you did in the other setting, you call on God.

Somehow, miraculously, I made my payroll.

We shouldn't save faith as our last hope in the wilderness – it can be the steady guide for all of our actions. The ability to face the impossible is available to us all the time. Faith does not have to be our spare tire; it can be our steering wheel. The entrepreneur who walks on the spiritual path lives a life of faith in action, grounded with a spiritual connection, guided by integrity, and unaffected by fear. They have moved from fear to faith.

There is an exhilaration and ease that accompanies acting in faith. When we are acting in faith, it can be said that we are operating in the "flow." It is the same flow felt by peak performers at the top of their game. Flow is that "can't lose" feeling where nothing seems impossible. It feels as if you are a medium for a larger force. You sink the bucket or hit the hole in one, in part because you are connected to something that doesn't know how to miss the bucket or the perfect golf shot. The flow engages you on every level – by disengaging your sense of self.

Mihaly Csikszentmihalyi, an author, former department chair of psychology at the University of Chicago, and director of Quality of Life Research Center at the Drucker School of Management at Claremont Graduate University has spent more than 25 years researching the concept of flow. He describes flow as a state of intense emotional involvement and timelessness that comes from immersive and challenging activities. [Flow is]"being completely involved in an activity for its own sake. The ego falls away. Time flies. Every action, movement, and thought follows inevitably from the previous one, like playing jazz. Your whole being is involved, and you're using your skills to the utmost."

The Autotelic Personality of the Entrepreneur

Flow is harnessed when we are actively involved in a difficult enterprise, in a task that stretches our mental and physical abilities. The entrepreneurial path is uniquely suited to deliver continuous flow. The tension between risk and reward, the challenge of creation and the sense of adventure all contribute to the complexity and difficulty of heading a business enterprise. We can become absorbed and lose ourselves in the process.

Csikszentmihalyi's research also distinguishes the "autotelic" personality. Autotelic derives from two

Greek words, "auto" meaning self, and "telos" meaning goal. It refers to a self-contained activity, one that is done not with the expectation of some future benefit, but simply because the act of doing is itself the reward. The essence of the autotelic person is that he or she is living a life guided by choice. The power of choice is the engine of the entrepreneur. It is the motivator and the muse. The self-direction and focus required of successful business owners aligns with the characteristics of the autotelic personality.

The Flow Experience in a Spiritual Context

The flow experience is distinguished by several characteristics that are consistent with the concept of operating in the spiritual path.

Elements of the Spiritual Path	Faith in action (through difficulty) ...	... grounded with a spiritual connection...	... guided by integrity ...	... unaffected by fear.
	⇕	⇕	⇕	⇕
Characteristics of Flow	A challenge requiring skills	Deep involvement transcending distractions	Medium for a larger force	A sense of control over actions

Faith in Action

Action requires movement on a particular task. Faith in action is more likely to be employed when that task involves a challenge. Faith is not something we think about when we wash the dishes or walk the dog. Faith guides our path when we are making a critical presentation to investors or trying to land a new customer. Tasks involving a raised and balanced level of challenges and skills are the basis of the flow experience.

Grounded with a Spiritual Connection

Flow facilitates the "expansion and absorption" of the self. When we are connected to Source, the highest level of communion, time does not exist. We touch the Eternal. We know that the self can be expanded through time and absorbed in the Divine when we are with the one we love. It can also happen when we are performing the work that we love. Sustained flow states allow us, through our connection with Spirit, to produce without being constrained by time. An hour's worth of results can be created in fifteen minutes. In flow, the miraculous occurs naturally. In truth, we were born to live our lives in the flow.

Guided By Integrity

When a high performer receives an "A-" on a term paper, her next question is "What does it take to get an A+?" This seeking of integrity pushes us to extend single moments of flow into long-term success. Focus on our goals and feedback allows us to measure our progress and to adjust our performance to continue in the flow.

For entrepreneurs, there are measures that are built into business ownership that automatically provide goals and feedback. Income statements, balance sheets, cash flow statements and sales results help us to adjust skills to meet the challenges of running a business. Accountability for results is a critical part of the infrastructure for personal integrity, and it can create success for a business. As business owners, we can sometimes over-emphasize activities related to vision and idea generation, but integrity and accountability keep the business alive. Vision enables companies to move to the next level; however that next level is unavailable to the business whose integrity is compromised.

"As an entrepreneur, you're always accountable to someone," says Domineca Neal. "People tend to think accountability ends once you own a business. Actually, you are more accountable because you put your finances and emotions on the line. I have to talk about my vision on a whole different level than when pursuing a professional job. It actually exposes you completely as you become more accountable to lenders and partners."

Unaffected By Fear

There is an incredible sense of control that comes from not resisting (or feeding) fear and allowing it to simply be. Fear is an important part of faith in action. It triggers the adrenaline and heightens the senses. It lets us know that we are walking in territory that requires us to lean on God to make it through.

While fear serves its purpose to prepare us to act, it does not affect the action itself. Fear is not an integral part of flow. When we are in flow, fear is at best a footnote to the experience. We can be nervous and fearful before speaking to the decision makers on a major contract. We can even be shaken afterwards, but when we act, fear falls away. It becomes a theoretical concept whose power is drained by the lack of ego to feed it.

Success vs. Flow

Success is the goal of enlightened entrepreneurship. There are some who feel happy about their work -life balance, yet they never find the financial reward they originally set out to achieve. There are others who are building their bank accounts, yet they are draining their own life force. Writer and award-winning cyclist Barclay Brown says,

> *Successful businesspeople and entrepreneurs are not always in flow, nor are those in flow always successful. The successful who are not in flow experience dissatisfaction with their work, and have the symptoms of so-called "Type-A" personality disorders--ulcers, anxiety, heart attacks and the like. Those in flow but not successful know that they are not yet successful by the measurements they themselves have set up, and are anxious only in the same sense as an athlete nervous before the big game. Indeed, the physical sensations of anxiety and excitement are identical -- the only difference is the mental attitude that accompanies them.*

Flow is the positive experience; success is the positive result. Flow without success and success without flow are unacceptable compromises. Flow and success can and should co-exist.

Toolkit

The flow experience is faith in action, grounded with a spiritual connection, guided by integrity, and unaffected by fear. Describe the last three instances of flow you felt as an entrepreneur. What were the conditions that led operating in flow? Are you able to put yourself in flow at will? How did you know you were operating in flow? How did operating in flow feel? How do you define success? Did operating in flow lead to success?

Instance #1	
Instance #2	
Instance #3	

Finding Flow

List your interests and your passions. For each, describe why they interest you and how much time you spend doing them. Jot down any insights you gained from this exercise and be prepared to share them with your Core.

Homework

Meditation

A pilgrimage, after all, is a strenuous
undertaking, one in which companionship and
support may be pivotal.

Julie Cameron

There are only two ways to live your life:
as though nothing is a miracle, or as though
everything is a miracle.

Albert Einstein

Questions to consider

1 Have you achieved success?

2 How can the concepts we have discussed in this book be applied to your business and your life?

3 Are you willing to recreate your business and your life?

4 What do you notice about the conversation you had with yourself when answering the questions above?

Step 10:
Walk the Path

The entrepreneur must walk the spiritual path daily, living by choice and by faith. It is not easy, nor is it clear-cut. In choosing this path, you are choosing the opportunity to grow. That growth requires effort, strength, fortitude, wisdom, openness to learning, and a willingness to make mistakes. It also requires contribution from others and sharing of ourselves.

"Everybody you encounter should be blessed as a result of that encounter," says Rogers Foster, a Detroit-based professional photographer. "How do you do that? It's particularly in your attitude, the products you deliver and the way you deliver them."

The Structure

Over the last nine lessons, you have studied each of the steps of the spiritual path. You have reinforced that study with exercises, homework and discussion. Now is the time to build the structure that you need on your daily walk. This structure should integrate each of the ten steps and bring focus to your destination. Below are several guidelines that will help you to build a system that works.

Make It A Game

Throughout history, the games that we humans have created have captured our attention and imagination. Games inspire us, challenge us, frustrate us and thrill us. We can become immersed in a game, lose the game and keep playing without hesitation because it is just a game. We have put those activities in the realm of play. When we are at play, we are free to fail or succeed as many times as we like without it affecting our sense of self. We are committed to winning, but not overly attached to it. Therefore, the realm of play is the ideal domain to build the structure for your path.

Create An Inspiring Goal

As you create the game, remind yourself frequently of the overriding purpose that drives your efforts. The goal should be in the form of a short vision statement that conveys the ultimate outcome of the game. An example is, "The goal of my game is to be paid plentifully for my passion."

Create Rules

Rules are a sort of self-policing system that needs to be

explicit in order to be effective. The rules of your game will be its cornerstone and its guiding integrity. As you develop your game, you should ensure that the rules are comprehensive enough to help you generate the results you desire.

Follow The Rules And Keep Score

The most challenging and fulfilling games have rules that are clear and rigid because measuring the level of adherence provides valuable feedback. Keeping score adds consequences and makes the game real. Your ability to maintain your path will be highly dependent on your ability to follow the rules and keep score.

Create A Team for Feedback

If your game only existed in your head, then it would not be real. There would be no accountability and no evidence that the game existed. A team can help you in a variety of ways: providing valuable feedback, being a support system, adding needed expertise in areas where you may not be as knowledgeable, holding you accountable to your results, and continuing to help you refine the game.

Set Goals Projecting Outcomes

Focusing on future outcomes and working toward their completion ensures forward movement. Begin by developing a specific desired future and logically determining the required steps necessary to achieve them. Start from where you are now. In order for this process to work, you must be completely honest about your current position. For example, if you are not generating the income you want, you can only start to change it by recognizing where you actually are today.

Allocate Resources To Achieve Results

Time, money and people are the basic resources for any endeavor, and the game that you are creating is no different.

Time: The needed time involvement should be planned, whether it is daily, weekly, monthly or quarterly.

Resources: The assets you need for your game should also be noted. There will also be expenses, both short term and long term.

People: The people you will need include the team that directly works to generate results and the people who will serve a more indirect role. If you are playing your game for a high-level goal, there are people you need to have conversations or relationships with that you do not currently know.

Plan for all of these resources and get creative about how they might be used.

Track Your Progress

As you progress on your path, track your wins and your losses in order to learn from them. Tracking your progress gives you a wider perspective on the game you have chosen and allows you to continually refine it to meet your needs. There are times when we create results in our lives and have no idea how they were generated. Tracking your progress helps you to link your actions with your results so that you can gain the ability to reproduce those results intentionally and consistently.

Surrender To The Process

As entrepreneurs, we are sometimes turned off by the idea of structure and process, preferring instead to focus on generating the next big idea. The process of staying on the spiritual path requires surrender to the structure. That means following the rules, even when they are inconvenient. By surrendering to the process, we work from our commitments, rather than our impulses. The results that occur from committed play are dramatically different than the results we chance upon when only halfway playing the game.

Keep Playing

The game of the spiritual path, like the game of life, can be a source of incredible insight and spiritual growth. There are times when that growth is either too overwhelming to digest or too subtle to notice. There are times when it seems that the structure is not working for you. You are invited to play the game anyway, for the love of the game. Wake up everyday choosing to play, and you will experience the power of that choice.

My Game Structure

Following is a sample structure for staying on the spiritual path. It is a useful guide for building your structure to maintain yourself on the spiritual path; however, your structure should reflect your own goals and needs.

The Business Plan

Vision Statement	Entrepreneurship as an expression of faith
Specific, Measurable Goal	I will develop and pilot a seminar on the spiritual path of the entrepreneur by December.
Time	Saturdays from 6pm to 8pm; Sundays from 11am to 4pm

Resources	Expenses	
	Course materials	200.00
	LCD projector	1,500.00
	TOTAL	1,700.00
	Assets Available for Game	
	Laptop with Microsoft PowerPoint Web site	
	<u>New Assets Required</u>	
	LCD projector	
People	*Reviewers* Alicia Nails (writing) Nikki Cole (spiritual context) *Partners* Marilyn French Hubbard (training expert)	

Success Metrics

Success Measurement	1. Existence of seminar 2. % of positive reviews of seminar
Opportunities to Maintain My Personal Integrity During the Process	• Build my own spiritual structure • Ensure proper use of all supplementary materials

Milestone Chart

This chart is constructed to begin from the future, working backwards into the present. It is designed this way to keep the ultimate goal at the front of my thinking, and to let everything else be driven by the goal.

December	November	October
Conduct course *Evaluate performance*	*Conduct focus group on pilot course* *Secure permissions*	*Conduct pilot course*

September	August	January-July
Secure sales partner *Finalize pilot course*	*Create spiritual structure* *Finalize first draft of course materials*	*Design course*

The strides you make in your spiritual path will serve you far beyond the domain of your business life. You will gain insights into your love relationships, your family, and your health – along with a richer knowledge of your faith and your business. Faith is not intended to be separate from any aspect of your life. God is everywhere. This path allows you to feel God's presence, to participate in co-creation of the business you envision and to achieve the success you desire. You have the opportunity to live life fully and to experience the abundance that is your birthright–claim it!

Our role as humans is to realize our connection to our Source and to each other. The movement from fear to faith is the primary lesson that we have all been sent here to learn.

Toolkit Index

Recommended Web Sites

fromfeartofaith.com

aspeninstitute.org

chopra.com

evolve.org

gladwell.com

hayhouse.com

innervisionsworldwide.com

malidoma.com

marianne.com

meditationsociety.com

myss.com

onethemovie.org

opencenter.org

oprah.com

richdad.com

santafe.edu

spirituality.com

theartistsway.com

thecorporation.tv

thesecret.tv

unity.org

whatthebleep.com

Recommended Readings

The Bhagavad Gita

The Bible

The Talmud

The Torah

The Qur'an

Anderson, U.S. *Three Magic Words*. Wilshire Book Company, 1980.

Bach, Richard. *Illusions: The Adventures of a Reluctant Messiah*, Dell Publishing Company, 1994.

Cameron, Julie. *The Artist's Way: A Spiritual Path to Higher Creativity*, 10th anniversary edition. Jeremy P. Tarcher, 2002.

Csikszentmihalyi, Mihaly. *Finding Flow: The Psychology of Engagement with Everyday Life*. BasicBooks, 1997.

Ephirim-Donkor, Anthony. *African Spirituality: On Becoming Ancestors*. Africa World Press, 1997.

Foundation for Inner Peace. *A Course In Miracles*, Foundation for Inner Peace; 1975.

Gardner, Chris and Quincy Troupe. *The Pursuit of Happyness*. Amistad, 2006.

Gerber, Michael. *The E-Myth Revisited: Why Most Small Businesses Don't Work and What to Do About It*, HarperCollins, 1995.

Gibran, Khalil. *The Prophet*. Alfred A. Knopf, 2002.

Hay, Louise. *Heal Your Body: The Mental Causes for Physical Illness and the Metaphysical Way to Overcome Them*, Hay House, 2002.

Readings (continued)

Holms, Ernest. *The Science of Mind*, reprint edition. Jeremy P. Tarcher, 1998

Hubbard, Marilyn French. *Sisters Are Cashing In: How Every Woman Can Make Her Financial Dreams Come True.* Perigree, 2000.

Johnson, Spencer. *Who Moved My Cheese?* G.P. Putnam's Sons, 1998.

Kiyosaki, Robert T. *Rich Dad Poor Dad: What the Rich Teach Their Kids About Money – That the Poor and Middle Class Do Not!* TechPress, Inc., 1998

Montilus, Guérin. *Dompim: The Spirituality of African Peoples.* Nashville: Winston-Derek Publishers.

Shinn, Florence Scovel. *The Game of Life and How to Play It.* Lushena Books, 2001

Some, Malidoma Patrice. *Of Water and the Spirit: Ritual, Magic, and Initiation in the Life of an African Shaman,* reprint edition. Penguin Books, 1995.

Some, Malidoma Patrice. *The Healing Wisdom of Africa: Finding Life Purpose Through Nature, Ritual, and Community.* Jeremy P. Tarcher, 1999.

Tsu, Lao. *Tao Te Ching, 25th anniversary edition.* Vintage Books USA, 1997.

Vanzant, Iyanla. *One Day My Soul Just Opened Up: 40 Days and 40 Nights Toward Spiritual Strength and Personal Growth.* Fireside, 1998.

Williamson, Marianne. *A Return to Love: Reflections on the Principles of "A Course in Miracles",* reissue edition. Perennial Currents, 1996.

About the Author

Marlo Rencher started her entrepreneurial career cutting lawns with her brother during the hot summers of the early eighties. With over a decade of entrepreneurial experience, Ms. Rencher has launched or managed five companies including a digital marketing firm and a publishing and media company. She and her husband own an education services company.

A Michigan State University graduate, she sold cereal for Kellogg, marketed Kool-Aid Bursts for Kraft and researched cars and trucks for Ford. She graduated from the MBA program at the University of Michigan Business School. She is a doctoral candidate in business and organizational anthropology at Wayne State University. Her research interests include design anthropology and the rituals of online communities. She has both domestic and international consulting experience, having worked on projects based in Frankfurt, Germany; Paris, France; and Johannesburg, South Africa.

A trained business coach, Marlo Rencher has guided scores of entrepreneurs through the peaks and valleys of business ownership. *From Fear to Faith: 10 Steps on the Spiritual Path of the Entrepreneur* is her first book.